THE TELEVISION COMMERCIAL

COMMUNICATION ARTS BOOKS

THE TELEVISION

COMMERCIAL

HOW TO CREATE AND PRODUCE

EFFECTIVE TV ADVERTISING

BY

HARRY WAYNE McMAHAN

HASTINGS HOUSE PUBLISHERS
NEW YORK

Printed in the United States of America

Library of Congress Catalog Card Number: 54-9883

Published simultaneously in Canada
By S. J. Reginald Saunders, Publishers, Toronto

ACKNOWLEDGMENTS:

I am indebted to the more than 200 advertising and film men throughout the country who read the pre-publication version of this book and made their suggestions and criticisms. They have helped to shape this work as their own.

My debt extends to the many Ad Clubs and trade publications who invited me to use them as sounding-boards for excerpts of this material.

Lastly, I am indebted to the viewer, whose name is Legion.

Mr. Legion sat through (most of the times, that is!) the 5,000 commercials that guinea-pigged this book. Better still, he went out and bought enough products and services to prove its yardsticks. He's a good Joe.

If this book be dedicated then, it is to our customer: Joe Legion.

May his standards of viewing and his standards of living both continue to improve.

HARRY WAYNE McMAHAN

July 1, 1954
50 Rockefeller Plaza
New York City

FOREWORD:

"Faces and Other Simple Objects"

The Fourteenth Edition of the Encyclopedia Britannica, published in 1929, contains these quaint comments:

> "In the same year (1928) several radio stations in the United States initiated the broadcasting of faces and other simple objects. Many technical problems have yet to be solved before television can claim to be more than an interesting novelty . . ."

Perhaps the predictions of today may sound as naive when they are reviewed twenty-five years from now. We shall probably be looking at three-dimensional television in color from all parts of the globe, and there may be as many television sets as there are radio sets today, or more.

But, if America continues to progress on the initiative and

competitive spirit of business, and if the world economy continues to be built on the capacity and appetite of people to consume the increasing amount of better goods which we are able to produce, then we shall still have with us the television commercial in the form of "faces and other simple objects" designed to sell these better goods in increasing quantities.

As a guide to the TV craftsman of today and as a solid base for future development, Harry McMahan has prepared this very practical book. He has taken a lot of the ghosts and the snow out of this "interesting novelty" called television.

He has pointed the way to more efficient expenditure of TV commercial dollars, and maybe even to an improved commercial culture in this vital country of ours where selling things and services and ideas to each other is part and parcel of our accepted, respected and dynamic way of life.

LEO BURNETT

CONTENTS

INTRODUCTION

The television commercial has now reached adolescence and needs to face the facts of life.

In the early days, this brash youngster never had to work very hard to earn a living. Even with hit-and-miss techniques, people liked him and people bought.

Now comes the awkward age. The youthful charm is gone and the familiar childish tricks no longer satisfy the rising cost of his selling job. Obviously, maturity demands a better integrated knowledge of advertising and production techniques for the man-sized sales work ahead.

What steps can be taken to be more certain of success? What yardsticks can help pre-judge a commercial?

To plan for the future, we need to study and analyze the past. Both success and failure are good teachers and, by now, television has had its share of each and is ready to start an evaluation.

Success has helped to find the yardsticks.

Failure has also helped. Failure has proved that the production of a good commercial is only part of the job.

Like a good radio spot or a good newspaper ad, a television commercial must reach the correct pre-selected audience and it must have complete support in merchandising, from packaging to point-of-sale. Advertising, as always. is only part of the job.

Since 4 out of 5 of the television commercials used by major agencies now are on film, it is well to point out that this book concerns itself primarily with the creation and production of *film* commercials.

It considers both fact and theory. It studies both ideas and mechanics. We know successful advertising begins with an *idea*. In television, we discover this *idea* succeeds in ratio to creative and production values.

This book then, deals with the successful ideas of advertising men, the yardsticks that measure those ideas in this new medium, and the production techniques that develop those ideas into bettter television commercials that *sell*.

THE TELEVISION COMMERCIAL

CHAPTER 1

Television As a Selling Tool:

Sight and Sound

There are two basic kinds of advertising:

Advertising to be *seen*.
Advertising to be *heard*.

Television is both.

THE SENSE of sight and the sense of sound have long worked their independent ways to do effective selling. The billboard is effective. Radio is effective.

It follows that television, with both sight and sound, should be more effective. Plus this fact: The sight is *sight-in-motion*.

The United States Navy concludes from its audio-visual tests that you absorb 35% more when sight is used along with sound. And you retain this knowledge 55% longer.

You absorb more, you retain it longer. It is doubly vivid.

1

Those are two advertising superiorities of a good television commercial: 1) its impact on your mind is more informative and convincing and 2) you are more apt to carry its persuasion until the time you have an opportunity to buy the product.

STEP-BY-STEP CONTROL

There is still another great advantage in television: *You can control the sales story as it develops, step-by-step, to the final persuasion.*

Good personal salesmanship requires opening attention, full interest, point-by-point sales development and forceful closing.

A magazine or a newspaper ad, for instance, cannot control these factors, since the casual reader may start at any one point in the ad and completely miss other points which are vital to the selling job.

A television commercial can control these factors, step-by-step and point-by-point, and the viewer then gets the correct sales story in logical sequence.

It is true that many commercials still neglect to utilize this powerful advantage to the fullest. But the potential still exists: the opportunity to convey a controlled, step-by-step sales message.

WHAT ARE THE DISADVANTAGES OF TV?

Television may not be the best medium for every advertiser. It has its disadvantages. Especially, TV is:

1. Expensive. If you lack the budget, or if you are too faint-hearted, TV is not for you.
2. Wasteful. Your product may not have a fair return potential in this medium. It is easy to miss your true audience.
3. Fleeting. Your message passes with the sweep of the second hand—and does not give your audience a *second* look . . .

Further: Viewers resent poor commercials. Viewers are

getting smarter. Competition is keener. And the day of the low-priced commercial is gone.

WHAT ARE THE ADVANTAGES?

The advantages of TV are fairly obvious now to most advertisers. Repeating the points originally mentioned, TV is:

1. Powerful. Sound and sight-in-motion combine to do a doubly effective selling job.
2. Memorable. Your message can be designed to penetrate deeper, cling to the memory longer.
3. "Step-by-step." You can control the sales story, point-by-point, to its conclusion.
4. Dramatic. You can demonstrate the product, quickly, effectively to mass audiences as never before.
5. Personal. TV is face-to-face, person-to-person. You reach the family in the home.

Further: TV is now a fairly flexible medium. It can be made to fit into almost any advertising budget, from local to national; it can be scheduled for ten-seconds or an hour in length.

SIGHT VS. SOUND

Granted that sight and sound combined form a potent selling tool, which is more important? That is an old question, never completely answered.

The networks answer by giving a 75% rebate when the advertiser "loses" the picture; 25% when his message has no sound, because of network failure.

But the answer should vary with each commercial. Jingles and chant tracks place a high stress on sound. Demonstration films require more stress on the picture.

Generally, the visual is more important because sight is our most believing sense—and we are selling belief. And pictures are more emotional, probe deeper psychologically, than words.

"Don't tell me, *show* me", said the Chinese.

3

TELEVISION AS A SELLING TOOL

THE CHANGING TIMES

Times change and already the new medium offers newer problems. The novelty begins to wear off and the weak commercial no longer has that early advantage. Costs are rising and competition increasing.

Let's define the areas where the commercial must change with the times.

The move is away from:

1. Irrelevant "gimmick" openings.
2. Over-use of optical tricks.
3. Jingles-for-jingling sake.
4. Obviously paid "testimonials".
5. Extravagant claims, not substantiated.
6. Too-perfect results with product, obviously gained through film trickery.

The move is to:

1. Believability in honest claims.
2. Believability in demonstration of product.
3. Simple, useful information.
4. Better psychological understanding of the viewer.
5. Better public relations, building good will and loyalty.
6. Combatting rising costs of production.

The future holds an exciting challenge: we are only on the threshold of the potential of the television commercial as a selling tool.

THE MOVE IS ON . . .

Television commercials are constantly "on the move" through new techniques in art and production. The need is now to marshall all the creative and production forces more closely with advertising aims and viewer believability. From experience, certain axioms have been developed and an attempt is made, at the end of each of the chapters of this book, to illustrate these in a "do-and-don't" form.

DO keep demonstrations simple and believable. Be honest in the actual demonstration, without camera tricks or exaggerated results. Work in closeups when possible so that the viewer learns by example how to use the product correctly.

DON'T have exaggerated situations and dialogue. Viewers spot them as "phony" and then will not believe your later claims. Demonstrations must always stay within the practical experience of viewers or they are inclined to reject the commercial.

DO present your product in all its "visual worth". Good camera work, good lighting can "clothe in value" and give unspoken superiorities to your product. Validate each claim visually with honest pictorial proof.

DON'T make wild claims you cannot prove. TV exaggerates the exaggerated claim—more than any other media—and makes it ridiculous. Surveys show viewers particularly reject the extravagant claims made for cosmetics and cigarettes.

CHAPTER 2

The Eleven Men On The Team:

Position and Goal

WHEN A television commercial gets kicked around, it is well to remember that 11 men are primarily concerned with its creation and any *one* can fumble the ball.

Behind the 11 men are many more on the sidelines. Often 100 different persons, including 20 crafts and unions, will work on a single minute's film.

At least 7 of the basic 11 men must have *creative skill* as well as *technical skill*. The hazard is great if their interpretive talents are not carefully guided and coordinated toward the desired result.

In practically all other forms of advertising, only technical skill is required from suppliers outside the advertising agency. Compositors, engravers, printers and other craftsmen supply services in established known quantities, meeting set standards.

Not so in television commercials, for at least 6 of the 7 creative craftsmen come from outside the agency.

POSITIONS OF THE TEAM

Obviously, all must work as a team, and here is how they line up:

The backfield

FB
The Advertiser

HB
Account Executive

HB
Agency TV Director

QB
Creative Writer

The line

E	T	G	C	G	T	E
Actors	Editor	Director	Producer	Cameraman	Lab	Voices

The comparison with football is not as far-fetched as it may sound. It takes "team spirit", first in the backfield, then in the line. There must be strong field generalship. Communication of signals is vital. And any one of the 11 can be "off-side" or fail in his team assignment and spoil the play.

WHERE THE PLAY ORIGINATES

The backfield originates the commercial as the advertiser (sponsor) and two key advertising agency men, the account executive and the TV director, determine the need.

The creative writer is in the quarterback slot, the vital sparkplug who translates the determined need into a play most likely to reach the goal. He has to know what the 3 men behind him want and what the 7 men in front of him can do.

He may be a member of the agency staff or the producer's staff but, regardless, he is potentially the most important man on the team. He needs to know the functions of every other man on the team to get the best efforts from each, and he must communicate his ideas clearly, beyond misinterpretation.

THE ELEVEN MEN ON THE TEAM

In some larger agencies, the art director is teamed with the creative writer—an ideal collaboration in this audio-visual medium. The graphic mind of an art director, when it becomes conversant with production techniques and costs, can contribute much to the television commercial. All too frequently, however, the writer must work alone and then have his script translated to a story-board by some artist he never sees. This can be the beginning of trouble.

The detail and clarity with which a script is written affects the successful interpretation by the other creative men. Each scene and each action must be described so expertly that only one true picture is created as the various members of the team read it. A "second-string" quarterback can be costly, in every sense of the word.

THE LINE GOES INTO ACTION

The producer is the center of the line. He needs to be in the huddle as early as possible so he can suggest where his men might improve their efforts. The line is his responsibility.

Closest to him are the director (live or cartoon) and the cameraman. Both have valuable creative sparks to give to the writer's idea and it is important that they interpret this basic idea with the same objective, not as separate creative efforts.

On the ends are video and audio—the actors (live or cartoon) and the voices of the sound track.

The other two factors in the line are the editor and the laboratory. The editor, too, must have a clear, articulate understanding of the basic idea for his interpretation.

Only the lab has nothing creative to offer, but its technical skill has a vital bearing on the work of all others.

WHY SO COMPLEX?

The television commercial is complex because it is a creative effort with 6 different persons interpreting one basic idea.

Unfortunately, these 6 persons are all outside the advertising agency, and here television differs from other media.

12

The actor and the director have no set standards, as does the printer. Their interpretations are variables. The producer selects them on the basis of related experience, hopes to achieve a certain potential. The weakness of any one may ruin the strength of another.

The television commercial can never have exact, specified standards. Related experience can be the only judge, and that is why our concern in this book must be with such related experience.

CALL THE SIGNALS CLEARLY

Faulty communication of ideas is one of the prime causes of poor television commercials.

If the script has not told the whole story, if it has not created the *same* basic mental picture in the minds of the entire team, it has failed. The variance of individual interpretations will ruin it.

At the same time, the weak script that gets "added thoughts" and format changes from the advertiser, the account executive and others, is a fumble from the start.

The writer actually must be a "man with four heads", knowing the business of writing, of advertising, of film techniques—and to be most useful he must also know the cost of each scene and the multiple SAG talent payments.

Most of all, he must know how to write clearly, so that the rest of the team, and consequently his audience, understands him.

So much for the writer and the eleven men. More of this later, especially in Chapter 15. But now let's go on down to the other end of the field and take a look at the goal: the viewer.

DO be natural. Here both the direction and casting are improved. It's refreshing to see a middle-aged woman and a slightly balding man. The action draws interest to the product in a warm and friendly way and says, "More coffee?"

DON'T be stilted. The director has a definite creative spark to give the actors in staging and "business". Here the cast is obviously uncomfortable — a psychological factor that translates in negative fashion to the viewer.

DO cast for believability. Often it is wise to use the older housewife in "example" selling. Authority begins at 40, as Kate Smith, Arthur Godfrey and others prove. So never trade glamor for authority in your TV commercial.

DON'T cast for beauty. The pretty girl does not have the place in a TV spot she has in the magazine ad. The magazine reader can leisurely transfer his attention to the copy— but the TV viewer may never get his mind off the pretty girl.

VIEWERS HAVE looked long enough at the television commercial until now it's time for the commercial to start looking at the viewers.

There was no hurry to study the viewer of the early days of TV because enough people liked what they saw and bought what they liked. Anything sold anyone.

The viewer hardly knew how it happened. He was soft-soaped by slick sophistry, tricked by pitchmen, captured by "gimmicks" and finally got lost in a mass of extravagant, conflicting claims.

Slowly he is showing a tendency to lose his gullibility and build up a defensive barrier against false advertising. Surveys indicate he doesn't believe three-fourths of those cigarette claims and his wife doesn't believe one-half of the cosmetic claims.

Yes, the viewer is getting smarter with every station break.

THE WHEELS SPIN FASTER

Television is making the consumer *wiser* far faster than radio ever did. In the last 50 years, the spread of general knowledge to our mass population has accelerated through better newspapers, magazines, the movies and radio, in turn.

Television throws it into overdrive.

As knowledge increases, the personal defensive barrier toughens against advertising's cruder attacks. Housewives doubt that movie stars really use all of those products they endorse. Men doubt there are startling differences in gasolines. Youngsters learn their sports heroes get paid for testimonials.

TV Exaggerates the Exaggerated Claim

Advertising claims have almost reached the point of no return, but it took television to underline the problem. Quite obviously, the added impact of television makes the exaggerated claim more exaggerated, and the viewer rebels.

Philip Morris switched more than a million smokers with their "nose test" TV campaign, but the gain was short-lived, for this cigarette dropped from 4th to 5th place in sales the following year.

We need to be simple, honest, informative, believable. And we need to better understand the viewer, emotionally, in his reactions.

HIS NOSE IS COUNTED — AND DISCOUNTED

Statistical research is now trying to dissect the viewer, tabulating his likes and dislikes, electronically recording his "yes" and "no" and counting his nose every time he lifts it from the set.

The viewer replies only with what his neighbors and every red-blooded American advertising man expects of him.

Sure, he likes Schlitz beer, wants to own a Cadillac, admires Betty Furness, knows the words to "Pepsi-Cola hits the spot . . ." and recalls a dozen advertising slogans (tagging many of them to the wrong product).

He wants to be a good Joe. And he doesn't want the interviewer to consider him "different" from his neighbors, unless that little difference is a superiority!

Much of this statistical research on the viewer is superficial and only proves what the researcher was hoping to prove. But don't count noses and expect to know men's minds.

Unless you probe deeper into the mental processes and emotional reactions of the viewer, you'll never find his true attitudes

20

toward your product and those strange unconscious motivations that cause him to buy it—or reject it.

CLINICAL VIEW OF THE VIEWER

Psychological and sociological research are doing much to open the field beyond the viewer's superficial barriers. Both have helped our own school of experience in this analysis, and we are indebted to three research groups in particular:

Dr. Ernest Dichter, head of the Institute for Research in Mass Motivations, Inc., is noted for his introduction of the psychiatrist's "depth interview" in studying consumer emotional attitudes in advertising. His work is outstanding in the psychological field of advertising.

Dr. Burleigh Gardner and Harriett Moore of Social Research, Inc., have pioneered in the advertising study of Lloyd Warner's six social classes in America. They have pin-pointed "Mrs. Middle Majority", the composite housewife who represents the so-called American "mass market". Their work combines sociological and psychological concepts for the study of consumers and their motivations.

Dr. Herta Herzog and her colleagues in research at McCann-Erickson, Inc. have added the use of clinical personality tests to find out why a particular brand attracts its customers and who among current non-users represents its best prospects. Their work has been focused on the creative problems of advertising and the delineation of appeals likely to expand a brand's share of market.

PROFILE OF TODAY'S TELEVISION VIEWERS:

These three research groups have studied today's television viewers at length. From their separate studies, our own experience joins in agreeing on the following 12 points:

1. Viewers are wide open for messages that are personal, that mean "you". This is basic advertising, but television makes it

21

even more personal. Show how your product fits into their own lives and experiences.

2. The viewer's world begins with family. The man wants to be loved and respected by his wife and children. And she wants recognition for her job of holding the family together and satisfying their basic needs at reasonable cost.

3. Viewers are wishful about success, but in a small way: a little higher pay, a little better school for the children, a nicer home. Products and advertising that propose to elevate far out of class in one leap are discounted as unrealistic.

4. Viewers are not static. Basic emotional hungers have not changed, but "experience" has. Today, only one person in four can remember growing up without radio. Only one person in three can remember growing up without sound movies.

THINGS THAT MAKE THEM DEFENSIVE

5. Viewers resent negative attacks on their way of life and habits. They want to change and improve, but don't try to "shame" them out of their old ways or they'll resist.

6. Viewers are outspoken against four things in TV commercials: extravagant claims, artificiality in all its forms, bull-headed repetition, and "talking down". Don't insult their intelligence.

7. Viewers do not want to be *told*—they want to be shown, tactfully. They want to know how to do things, how to improve, but they don't want to ask, and often won't read directions. Let them absorb it "through the pores" as interested bystanders, not as students being taught.

8. Viewers are sometimes confused as to which product you are advertising and what it will do. That fault often is yours, because you try to crowd too fast. So keep it simple; repeat skillfully; fasten your brand name on securely.

THINGS THAT SPARK THEM

9. Viewers are interested in NEWS: new products, new features, new uses, new benefits. But they are sometimes skeptical

of anything *too* new, if it doesn't relate to something old that is already known. Use the known to sell the unknown. The viewer wants to be conversant with what's going on. He wants to be as smart—or smarter —than his neighbor.

10. Viewers love "bargains", but don't want to be known as "penny-pinchers". Boom years have made them forget the last depression and they are—to a certain degree—on a "live-for-today" kick, looking for fun, for pleasure, for comfort, for easy living—as long as the penalties aren't too great.

11. Viewers want convincing sales arguments, despite the fact they don't like obvious "high pressure". They really want you to help them "make up their mind"—but do it in such a way that they can rationalize that they have made it up themselves.

12. Finally, viewers have become pretty good judges of the "atmosphere" and quality of the commercial. They judge you by the caliber of your presentation. If it shows thoughtfulness, it would seem you try to please your customers. Remember, they are pretty wise about photographic trickery, so keep your demonstration honest. They pride themselves on being able to spot "phoneys", so avoid insincerity in all its forms.

YES, SMARTER THAN YOU THINK

That's how today's average television viewers feel about it. And their precocious children of this television age are sometimes 'way ahead of them. They're *all* smarter than you think.

But the wonderful thing about the viewers is this: They do accept the commercial as a necessary part of television, looking to it for information and advice on how to improve their way of life.

They look on the television commercial as "people" they know. There is a "personality" factor. Some are fun to be with. Some "exaggerate" and don't keep their promises. Some are helpful and trustworthy. Some are "old friends" and always welcome to drop in any time.

They classify commercials, unconsciously. And when they know them and believe them . . . they *buy!*

Cigarette commercials have only one chance in four of making their claims believed, according to a survey which reported 75% of the viewers negative to conflicting and exaggerated boasts in this field. Medical claims, particularly, are disbelieved.

24

Cosmetic commercials have only one chance in two with
the viewer, the same survey reports, since 50% of the television audience disbelieve the claims. The viewer is getting
smarter. Commercials must be more honest, more believable.

DO use familiar settings. This breakfast table and kitchen are within the desire-believability of the average viewer. Note the casting: This is a typical "Middle Majority" family. The family revolves around mother. The time she saves she spends doing more things for her family's happiness and welfare.

DON'T use settings beyond the experience of the viewer. In TV, the mind does not have time to orient itself to the unusual setting, then grasp the message. Social Research, Inc. questions this scene showing the housewife playing bridge with the time she saved by using this washer.

DO use wholesome feminine appeal. Call it "sex appeal" if
you wish, but keep it wholesome. Cosmetic commercials
frequently need this ingredient and it can be used intelli-
gently. The high gloss glamor types and "too pretty" girls
sometimes detract. It is best to use attractive types who win
on a "personality" basis.

DON'T flaunt sex on the television screen. Ill will impends for the advertiser who does not use good taste at all times in his TV commercials. The "V" no longer fits to a "T" and the lusty, busty days of Dagmar and Faye Emerson are no longer acceptable in the family circle. Advertisers are wise to impose their own censorship in advance.

CHAPTER 4

Start With The Idea:

Back To Basic Advertising

TO REACH the viewer, the first thing we need is the *idea*.

Successful advertising always deals in ideas. Behind the sale of any product must be the idea of what it will do for the person who buys it: a good, honest promise.

In ancient times, you might have given a sample of cheese to interest someone in buying your goat. Nowadays, in a more complex world, people buy more complex ideas that fit their needs.

The woman buys the idea that enriched flour means better health for her family. The man buys the idea that double-tube tires mean more safety for his children. The young girl buys the idea that this home permanent will mean greater popularity for herself.

"The simple fact of the matter, of course," says Marion Harper, "is that *ideas,* not things, are what people buy."

Always there must be the idea. It is the first principle of successful advertising in all media—and the principle all too often overlooked.

31

START WITH THE IDEA

IDEAS HIT AT FOUR TARGETS

The viewer, as we know him now, has many characteristics which television helped pattern. But, behind these, are four basic selfish motivations which are the "buying urges" to a S–A–L–E.

Self-preservation
Ambition
Love
Economy

The viewer looks at it this way:

Self-Preservation: Here's the first law of nature. I want food, clothing, shelter, health. Can you protect me from the problems and worries of life? Can you protect my health?

Ambition: This is what chases us from caves to skyscrapers. I want to be as good as my neighbors and then, I want to be a little better. Can you give me comfort? Ease? Convenience? Can you make me "belong"?

Love: I want to be loved. I want a mate and family. Can you help me keep the love of my family?

Economy: Now let's talk about money. Can you give me more value? Is your product superior to competition? Remember, I like "bargains", but I like to think I'm shrewd, not a "penny-pincher".

Yes, the viewer is basically selfish. That's advertising primer. Now, we need to shape the Idea to hit one or more of these targets.

WHERE DO IDEAS COME FROM?

The art of developing the idea with *imagination* is the creative phase of advertising. A good copy writer has *trained* imagination. He knows the limitations as well as the possibilities of his medium; he knows his advertiser's needs as well as his consumer's dimensions and desires.

The basic facts on a product which give rise to the idea can be found by simple research and logical reasoning.

32

Advertising has long had check list variations on these five sources of I–D–E–A–S:

Information of news value about the product.
Description of benefits of the product.
Experience of users of the product.
Advantages over competition.
$—cost or value.

THE CHECK LIST GOES TO WORK

Now, let's see how this might uncover an idea on your product.

Information of news value about the product: "Now in a new plastic bottle".

Description of benefits: "Convenient, easy to operate".

Experience of users: "Used and recommended by many young girls of the social set".

Advantages over competition: "Washes clothes whiter."

$—cost or values: "This car has sound value."

These are basic ideas, none very glamorous. Now comes the need for imagination.

WHERE DOES IMAGINATION COME FROM?

Imagination in advertising comes from *trained* creative thinking.

For instance, imagination sparked the five unglamorous ideas into these top ad-lines:

"Now in a new plastic bottle" . . .

"POOF! — THERE GOES PERSPIRATION!"

"Convenient, easy to operate" . . .

"NO SQUAT — NO STOOP — NO SQUINT!"

Self-PRESERVATION: Man first wants food and shelter, but this TV commercial for Celotex also hits ambition ("improve the looks"), love ("for your family") and economy ("low cost"). All four of these basic motivations stimulate the urge to buy.

Ambition: This is a secondary drive, not as powerful, but it does motivate buying. "Want to be a better cook?" asks Globe A-1. The same urge is appealed to with "It's easier . . ." and "Convenient recipes . . ." But be certain your customer's exact ambitions are known.

Love: Sex motivates the cash register, as all cosmetics advertisers are aware. But love, as an urge to buy, also includes the important love-of-family; also, the less important love-of-adventure. Because of its high emotional content, this often is mishandled.

Economy: "E" marks the start of *Economy* and the completion of SAL*E*—and few ads, TV or otherwise, overlook the urge of price and value. But the American public currently is far more interested in value than it is in price. Be certain in TV to prove value before you talk cost.

35

"Used by many young girls of the social set" . . .

"SHE'S LOVELY . . . SHE'S ENGAGED . . . SHE USES POND'S"

"Washes clothes whiter" . . .

"SHE HANGS THE CLEANEST WASH IN TOWN!"

"This car has sound value" . . .

"DOLLAR FOR DOLLAR, YOU CAN'T BEAT A PONTIAC!"

In every case, the imagination of the creative writer has stimulated the imagination of the consumer.

Imagination says "flavor" instead of "salt". It says "Accent" instead of "monosodium glutamate". Imagination *suggests* something without actually saying it. It stirs a picture in the mind's eye.

It is this graphic *picture quality* characteristic of imagination that makes it so vital in television advertising.

CHAPTER 5

Analysis and Aims:

Define Your Problem

THE BEST television commercials are designed to do specific jobs. They may vary in production techniques, length and cost according to an analysis of projected use.

The first thing is to carefully define your problem. Ask yourself three pertinent questions:

What are your overall sales objectives?

Who and where are your best customers?

How much can you profitably spend?

Television can be a shotgun or a rifle. It can hit close objectives and far ones, but you need to know your target before you load your gun.

Exactly where does television fit into your advertising picture? What are your overall sales aims?

Basic Sales Objectives:
1. Primary selling.
    a. Winning new customers.
    b. Holding repeat customers.
    c. Increasing use per capita.
    d. Showing old customers new uses.
2. Secondary selling.
    a. Forcing distribution.
    b. Helping present distribution.
    c. Improving manufacturer-dealer relations.
    d. Building sales-staff cooperation.
3. Institutional.
    a. Building brand name prestige.
    b. Increasing consumer "good will".
    c. Improving employee morale.
    d. Impressing stockholders.

Television can hit these targets, singly and in multiple, but the design of each commercial in your series must first take careful aim for best results.

PROGRAM VS. SPOT

Design also needs to take into account whether the commercial is to be used for program or spot.

In *program* usage, the advertiser selects and buys the type of entertainment vehicle desired for his messages. Programs run from 5 minutes to an hour or more in length and generally have stars and titles which become identified with the sponsor.

In *spot* usage, the commercial is sandwiched *between* two programs or, in some cases, it is one of a number of advertisers participating in a program selected and bought by the station or network.

Note that the word "spot" is also used in the trade to refer to a "spot market" or individual station, as distinguished from a network of stations. So it is technically correct to say that a *spot* announcement can be bought for either program or *spot* usage in a *spot* market.

Programs permit well-balanced planning of related commercials to do the overall selling job, while spots must stand on their own.

Budget is often the determining factor in the decision of program vs. spot. But not always.

Programs are desirable when:
1. A specific class or type of audience is desired.
2. Sponsor prestige insists.
3. Longer than :20 or 1:00 is desired to develop the sales message.
4. There is a "family" of products under single or related brand names.
5. The program and special merchandising will do a public relations job with the dealer or consumer.
6. A theoretical audience loyalty to the program might build a consumer loyalty to the product.

Spots are desirable when:
1. Flexibility is needed to handle each sales area.
2. Heavy "saturation" in a market is required.
3. Local competition is keen.
4. Local dealer tie-ins are desired.
5. Budget or the availability of broadcast time do not allow program.
6. SAG talent fees for programming are comparatively too costly.

It is rare when the same commercial format can serve both program and spot usage effectively.

WHO AND WHERE ARE YOUR BEST CUSTOMERS?

Statistical research gives you consumer analysis and market analysis. Some fortunate advertisers also have psychological and sociological research to tell them more about their viewers.

DO get the facts on your market and consumer. Lucky Tiger Hair Tonic, after the war, did research and found out the product was virtually unknown to men under 25. Result: a :20 jingle cartoon spot aimed directly at the butch-haired class. Such research is vital to better-aimed TV spots.

DON'T assume you know all about your consumer until you have qualified research on the subject. Ease and convenience may not be the primary reason the housewife wants to buy your coffee-maker. She may be looking for a foolproof way to make good coffee every time, so her husband will quit complaining.

ANALYSIS AND AIMS

Before you can design the best television campaign, you need to know who uses your product and *who doesn't;* who does the actual buying and who may influence the purchase. You need to know where your potential customer lives and what his social class characteristics are. When does he watch TV and what does he like on TV?

Research also can confirm your judgment on the main appeals of your product for this potential customer. Television has especial interest in "who may influence the purchase" because this is the medium that reaches the entire family at the same time. It can be a powerful factor in buying decisions.

Television has brought about family discussion of all advertised products as no other medium ever did before. Even the child has a vital voice in discussion, often as early as the age of three. With other media, this rarely has begun before the age of six.

"The child often takes great pride in knowing sponsors and products", points out Social Research, Inc. "Thus he demonstrates his increasing sophistication about the world around him".

Smart television commercials take advantage of this fact—because the child around the house often gives them an "extra broadcast" of slogans, catch-phrases and jingles. And, while the child is helping you sell the family now, he also is being molded as a future customer himself. Few products—even refrigerators and automobiles —can completely overlook the child in television advertising.

HOW MUCH CAN YOU SPEND?

It is imperative, with the rising costs of television, that we get the most for the client's advertising dollar. Sometimes the advertising dollar doesn't stretch far enough, and then television can point to its two added functions deserving of added budgets:

1. Television can do a prestige and public relations job, worthy of a special budget.

2. Television can do a pre-selling demonstration job, worthy of sales money. In today's supermarkets and other self-service operations, television can pre-sell the customer better than any other

medium. Television can replace the clerk, pre-answering questions, demonstrating, and offering personal selling arguments.

Those are the two "extra money" reasons for television when the matter of budget comes up.

THE COMMERCIAL BUDGET

The budget for the commercials should be set *before* the scripts are written. This can be determined on the basis of past experience and comparable quality desired or, if new to the medium, on either of two methods: 1) percentage-of-time or 2) cost-per-showing.

The first method allocates approximately 10% of time charges. In spot and local campaigns this may increase to 20% or even 25%. In high-billing network shows it may fall as low as 5%.

The second method computes the probable times the commercial will run, then figures the proportionate cost-per-showing. On a national network show, for instance, $500 is a likely cost-per-showing budget. Thus, if the commercial should figure to run 5 times, it can cost $2500. If it is good enough to run 13 times, then $6500 might conceivably be allocated for the production of the commercial.

Pabst Blue Ribbon's cartoon commercials on the *CBS Fights* cost $3000 each—but only $25 on a cost-per-showing basis.

Kellogg's Rice Krispies spent $3700 for a single cartoon jingle which ran 50 times on *Howdy Doody*. Cost-per-showing: less than $75.

Many other such instances exist, but most of these were before the Screen Actor's Guild required re-payments for talent on each network broadcast. These SAG payments sometimes require computation of a shorter life expectancy for the commercial.

THE MATTER OF REPETITION

How many times can a commercial be run without losing impact? What is the life expectancy?

We know that repetition increases viewer knowledge up to

DO expect long life where you have a variety of films in the same series. This Pabst Blue Ribbon TV jingle, one of 10, ran for more than two years. The varied treatments of the 10 films kept the series alive. Cost-per-showing: $25.

DON'T expect long life from a single film used in a heavy saturation campaign. This Kellogg TV jingle ran 50 times consecutively on *Howdy Doody* and, like a hit tune, burned itself out. However, it served its purpose and the cost-per-showing was only $75.

DO expect to repeat a singing jingle many times, especially in cartoon. This Wembley Tie spot ran intermittently for four years. Viewers do not quickly tire of music and animation, except iћ saturation campaigns, where repeated too often, too soon.

DON'T expect to repeat a live action film too often, particularly if it has characters or settings readily remembered. Viewers have a tendency to start finding fault with each new repetition of such scenes. Result: loss of believability.

a certain point, with cumulative results. Then indifference sets in and a "blocked reception" mentally awaits your broadcast. "At one point, repetition can result in psychological deafness and blindness", Dr. Ernest Dichter says.

Where is this point? There are many variables and we are far from having any method of measurement. These four factors seem to relate most directly to the life expectancy of a commercial:

1. Acceptability of content to the viewer.
2. Variety of films in same series.
3. Frequency of broadcast.
4. Technique employed (cartoon, live, etc.)

The "acceptability of content" does not refer to whether the viewer says he "likes" or "dislikes" the commercial, but whether the viewer finds a "reward", conscious or unconscious, for the time and effort he spends viewing the commercial. He may find it entertaining, informative, or in some way related to his personal experience and needs with a promise to satisfy.

Varied repetition helps. All films in a series should repeat the identical central theme for greatest impact, but variety in opening interest aids in stimulating viewer attention.

The frequency of broadcast can hasten "blocked reception". A spot, if well constructed, may be used intermittently for many months, or it can be killed in two weeks in a heavy saturation campaign.

The fourth factor in life expectancy is the production technique used. We will delve into this complexity in the next six chapters.

CHAPTER 6

The Five Production Techniques:

Costs and Comparisons

CHOOSE YOUR production technique to fit your problem, your product and your pocket-book.

The five production techniques available for television film commercials are:

1. Cartoon
2. Live Action
3. Stop Motion
4. Puppets
5. Photo Animation

Each technique has distinct advantages, best for specific objectives. Costs vary so that two or more techniques may be blended in the same commercial to control the budget.

The variance of costs between the different techniques—and within each technique—is one of the problems that is not easy to understand about this business.

One cartoon may cost $800, another $8,000. Live action may cost from $500 to $5,000. It is difficult to pin-point all the reasons, even as it is often difficult to explain all the variances in the cost of advertising art. Too many creative factors are involved.

THE FIVE PRODUCTION TECHNIQUES

YARDSTICK OF COSTS

Only from experience can we develop a yardstick. Here is a chart that is obviously controversial because it attempts to over-simplify a complex creative work.

PRODUCTION TECHNIQUE:	ADVANTAGES OF TECHNIQUES — Best For:	AVERAGE COST PER SECOND:
CARTOON	Gaining interest Trademark characters Personalizing product Exaggeration, fantasy Singing jingles	$80
LIVE ACTION (Narrative)	Demonstration Exposition Human interest Appetite appeal	$50
LIVE ACTION (Dialogue)	"Personality" commercials Testimonials Key copy lines	$60
STOP-MOTION	Demonstration Mechanical action Personalizing product	$40
PUPPETS	Trademark characters Singing jingles	$25
PHOTO ANIMATION	Special announcements Retouching products "Catalog" of products Signatures	$20

COST SPECIFICATIONS FOR CHART: Based on 1951-54 aver-ages of five commercial producers for national and regional adver-tisers. Full union labor operation in 35mm film original. Cartoons computed on "one-unit" animation; standing sets for live action. Films produced in series; if singly, allowing sufficient production time for combination with similar work to avoid waste and overtime. NOTE: Sound tracks and SAG talent payments extra.

Remember, there are many *exceptions,* but this chart can be useful to pre-set a budget for the creative writer or TV director. His knowledge of the variable cost factors within each individual technique can then accomplish the desired result.

WHAT THE CHART DOES NOT DO

The chart does not consider non-union or 16mm operations.

It is based on the competitive standards which national and regional advertisers must meet in television today.

It does not allow, in cartoon, for the animation of more than one primary character. Additional "units" cost extra, as the chapter on cartoon will explain.

It does not cover the cost of talent in live action and sound tracks under the 1953 SAG code which requires re-payments each broadcast on network programs and each quarter on spot campaigns.

It does not cover the cost of unusual settings and props, location trips or puppet dolls.

It does not cover that great bugaboo of the business: RUSH!

Rush delivery increases cost because of overtime payments, waste and the increased hazards for error. Time is money. Generally, live action is most economically delivered in 45-60 days, cartoon in 60-90 days. If you require live action in 21 days or cartoon in 30 days, it is obvious that the cost must go up.

IT'S LIKE BUILDING A HOUSE

The chart covers the normal preliminary estimates for national and regional advertisers.

It is similar to the architect's method of quoting you an average per-square-foot cost for frame, stucco, brick or other material, as you analyze your building problems and set a budget for your new home.

You may want brick, but the budget makes you settle for frame. And you may have to give up that extra bedroom you wanted. The architect then develops the blueprints to give you the best possible home for the budget.

The creative writer is like the architect. He must know how to get the most out of all the techniques, exactly what each does —and how.

Let's explore now each technique separately and find out more about these tools at our command.

DO use cartoon for exaggerated, comedy or fantasy types of people — better still for animals and for bringing inanimate objects to the screen. Certain trademark characters also can be animated with success. But remember that the cartoon world is never too logical.

DON'T waste cartoon treatment on normal people doing normal things. If there is no "exaggeration" in the face or body, it is extremely difficult to cartoon. Disney reanimated the Prince in *Snow White* but never was able to make the motions life-like. Further, cartoons of normal people are not as believable as live action.

DO use live action when you want to stir emotions. Where cartoon is "make believe", live action is within the viewers' own experience. Sometimes cartoon and live action can be blended—with a cartoon to open (it gains quicker interest) followed by live-action (it has more impact).

DON'T use cartoons for human interest. Cartoon kids are sometimes very cute—but if you want to get beneath the surface of your viewers' emotion, live action children are far more effective. Remember that the cartoon world is fantasy, exaggeration; comedy rather than humor.

CHAPTER 7

Cartoon:

The Universal Language

CARTOONS ARE the universal language, understood from Times Square to Timbuctoo. Cartoons are fun.

In television commercials, the animated cartoon has often the highest viewer interest, the longest life and the lowest cost-per showing. Yet it remains the most misused and abused technique in the business.

Cartoon is no cure-all. It has its limitations.

It wins quickest interest, but it lacks depth of penetration. In the movie theater, the audience likes and laughs at the cartoon, but it is emotionally moved by the live action dramatic feature. *Mickey Mouse* entertains, then passes from the mind, but *Dr. Jekyll and Mr. Hyde* tells a never-to-be-forgotten story which personally involves the viewer.

PSYCHOLOGICALLY SPEAKING

From a psychological standpoint, the cartoon is primitive, child-like in imagination. The cartoon is not *you*, it is someone else.

57

CARTOON

When it becomes too rational and tries to depict actual people in normal activities, it becomes unbelievable.

"Animation sacrifices credibility", reports an audience test comparing cartoon and live action commercials for Esso gasoline.

The cartoon always makes the viewer the bystander. He can see "the other fellow" in the cartoon situation, but he finds it difficult to picture himself. He never feels the personal involvement that he does in live action—and this is a clue to the failure of many cartoon commercials to do the best selling job in television.

"People enjoy the antics of cartoon characters but they don't believe them", said Leslie Harris regarding soap commercial believability. "As a result we always follow a cartoon commercial with real people doing the same thing and repeating the plug. Our tests have proved that only with such treatment are viewers sold on the product."

THE ADVANTAGES OF CARTOON

Experience teaches that the cartoon in television commercials is best for:

Gaining Interest, even as the flashing of a cartoon title on the screen wins theater applause. The S.O.S. *Magic Bunny* was built on this factor.

Trademark Characters, actual or devised. The Carnation "Milk Drop" is an example of a cartoon character devised to fit the product. Invariably, though, cartoon characters are better when animal-like than person-like.

Personalizing the Product, such as a car. A cartoon Ford can typify many models in used car commercials. Likewise a can of coffee or a jar of mayonnaise can be brought to life and given personality with a cartoon "face".

Exaggeration and Fantasy, because cartoon can stimulate imagination more broadly than any other technique. A fresh egg can fly to market. A dog can walk and talk like a man. The artist's pencil can be Aladdin's lamp.

Singing Jingles, because cartoon and rhythm go together like ham and eggs and the public does not readily tire of them. Cartoon jingles have the longest life expectancy of any type of television commercial.

THREE GRADES OF CARTOONS

There are three grades or sub-divisions in the cartoon technique: 1) full animation, 2) limited animation and 3) "grow" or "scratch-off" cartoon. Each grade decreases in cost—and effectiveness.

Full animation costs an average of $80 per second, but this may run as high as $200 per second on complex productions. As many as seven artists work on each frame of full animation and, since there are 24 frames required per second, 1,400 drawings may be required for a minute commercial.

What *moves* governs the cost of the cartoon, because more hand-labor is required as the amount of movement and the number of characters on the screen increase.

Most producers figure the cost of cartoons according to "units" of animation. If one simple character moves while the rest of the scene is static, it is "one unit". If two characters move at the same time, it becomes "two units". A quartet becomes "four units" and the price goes up.

HOW TO SAVE MONEY ON CARTOON

A wise animation director can save money in the layout of a commercial by concentrating animation at the points most vital to viewer interest and the sales story.

His knowledge—or the same knowledge in the mind of the creative writer—makes use of such devices as "cycles" and "free footage".

A "cycle" is repeat animation, such as a horse running in constant stride, parallel to the camera. The same sequence of pictures is photographed again and again. "Free footage" is a non-animated portion where the camera does the movement, such as moving along

59

CARTOON FOR OPENING INTEREST — The commercial that opens with cartoon wins immediate audience interest. The S.O.S. "Magic Bunny" was created for this reason, as it had to compete for attention on the *Show of Shows* variety bill.

FOR TRADEMARK CHARACTERS — A milk drop was appropriately animated for Carnation when TV came along. Trademark characters should be devised to fit the product and suggest its benefits, yet be simple to animate.

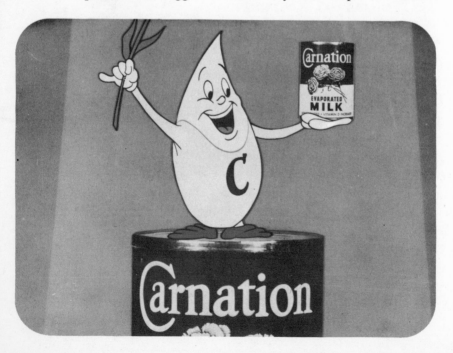

FOR PERSONALIZING THE PRODUCT — Cartoon is the ideal technique for giving the product a "personality". Here, for Ford service films, the cartoon car typifies all used cars, regardless of vintage. A cartoon face fits many products as well.

"GROW" TECHNIQUE — This type of cartoon animation, also called "scratch-off" is done by drawing the original picture on the screen, line by line. Whitman's used it to "grow" several appropriate "sampler" scenes on screen.

CARTOON

a static landscape to a house, where a door suddenly bursts open and the animation begins.

The planning of cartoons is the most complex, the least understood phase of the television commercial. Since few writers understand the potential cost factors, competent advice should be secured in the very earliest stages of planning.

CHEAPER GRADES OF ANIMATION

Limited animation costs about half as much as full animation. It is "limited" in the action and movement of characters on the screen. To be effective, its must make full use of "cycles" and "free footage". It often shows only extremes of expression and gives the illusion of action by dissolving or cross-fading in the camera from one extreme to the other. Camera movement is directed to the fullest and various lens tricks add to the effect.

Often limited animation scenes can be cut in with full animation to meet a given budget, but it must be planned ingeniously.

"Grow" cartoon cuts the cost in two again. This type of animation is also called "scratch-off", because it works with one single drawing, photographed in reverse as the lines are scratched off on successive frames. When projected in the opposite direction, the cartoon or sketch appears to "grow" or be drawn upon the screen.

The curiosity factor or "magical quality" of what the artist might be drawing is the secret of the success of this trick technique. But, when the drawing is completed, it needs to go into full animation or the viewer attention will wane as the movement stops.

WHEN CARTOON NEEDS LIVE ACTION SUPPORT

If your product is an "impulse" item or if you only require name identification, cartoon can do the job alone. But if the viewer must rationalize the buying of your product, cartoon needs the realistic support of live action. The two can be combined effectively.

Cartoon can gain interest and entertain, but it takes live

action to make the story believable and personalize it to the viewer's experience.

Demonstration films especially need to combine the two. However, all-cartoon spots can be made when the viewer already has been exposed to the necessary live action demonstration in previous commercials.

Pet Milk has used all-cartoon minute spots to supplement their live action series. Previous films had utilized live action to demonstrate Pet's three uses of infant feeding, cooking and creaming coffee. Then it was decided that cartoon could best combine all three uses in an imaginative saga of "Pet Milk Pete" and his story *I Grew Up on Pet*.

In the final analysis, remember: cartoons are fun. If you can sell your product with fun alone, then you can sell it with cartoon alone. If you need to get serious, if you need to convince, you had better back your sales story with live action.

CARTOON

The problem of this television commercial is to show in one happy cartoon the whole idea of the uses of Pet Milk tied up in one story: *I Grew Up on Pet!* The 3 uses: for infant feeding, for cooking, for creaming coffee, are all to be tied into the saga of "Pet Milk Pete". Pete is a swaggering, boastful western character, but he is completely lovable and quite the idol of kids. He tells the story, with flashbacks, in an easy-going doggerel style:

> I'm Pet Milk Pete, a rough, tough guy
> I'll shoot the whiskers off a fly —

SOUND EFFECT: PISTOL PING

> I lick my weight in wildcats, too
>> The reason why I give to you:
>>> I grew up on Pet!

WE NOW FLASH BACK TO PETE AS BABY:
> "Pet Milk!" the doctor said to me;
>> "A healthy lad needs Vitamin D!"

PETE, NOW 3 MONTHS, IN BASSINET:
> My bones got strong; my muscles . . . feel!
>> They had the spring of tempered steel!
>>> I grew up on Pet!

PETE, NOW 4 YEARS, AT SINK:
I out-grew that bottle like a calf
      Then switched to Pet, straight half-and-half
Pet's sweet country milk with the water taken out
      So I put it back in—right from the spout!
            I grew up on Pet!

PETE, NOW 10, BRANDING CALF "PET":
At 10, I was a real "top hand"
      I guess that you can guess my "brand"

PETE, NOW 12, WATCHING MOM COOK:
And all the time, Mom cooked with Pet —
      Those meals I never will forget.

PETE, NOW 18, PUNCHES COW IN NOSE:
At 18, I could punch a cow . . .
      I had my Pet with coffee . . . now!
            I grew up on Pet!

CUT BACK TO PETE AS HE OPENED:
So take my tip, for ol' Pete knows:
      That "whatcha eat is how you grows!"
So, grow up strong—the Pet Milk way!
      And have some Pet Milk . . . every day!

DO save cartoon money, when budget demands, by using such devices as "cycles". Here the horse is racing parallel to the camera. Only one complete stride needs to be animated, then this is photographed again and again as the background panel is moved behind it on the camera stand.

DON'T try to animate too many things simultaneously unless you have an unlimited budget. Cartoon costs are fig-
ured in "units", each unit meaning added labor to the seven
or more artists who work on the many successive drawings.
This scene with six bubbles singing is very expensive.

DO use cartoon trademark characters to win interest and develop high product identification. TV is doing more than any other medium to develop new cartoon trademark characters. However, remember live action is needed to do your primary selling job.

DON'T expect live action trademark characters to be as successful as cartoons. Problems include casting, voice, and SAG talent costs. In the case of Peter Pan Peanut Butter, live action was successful, giving added conviction to the sales story. But such live characters generally do not succeed.

The American public was raised on the Disney school of animation and this happy, easy-going style is always safest for television commercials. However, UPA started the modern trend in theater cartoons with *Gerald McBoing-Boing* and this technique has logically spread into the TV field. Favored by many art directors and "avant garde" disciples,

Disney-esque

Semi-Modern

70

it has gained steadily in popularity. Detractors claim that it is "neurotic", that it does not have the same widespread acceptance by the public as the Disney style of treatment. Following this is shown an abstract styling for television commercials which stirred up high interest in the trade, as reported by SPONSOR Magazine.

Abstract

Bouncing ball traversing the product name is used as a "logo" in series of abstract commercials. Ball bounces in time to music which is used as theme in the commercials

☆☆☆☆☆

'n art comes to commercials

Ludgin tv film commercial for regional coffee firm uses coordinated with well-timed music and narration

per-stamped tv commercials send kitchen for a refill.

usion Earle Ludgin and Co. came ago while planning a series of tv heir Midwest regional client, Mc-House Coffee. The Chicago agen-Look for television commercials.

n these pages from a McLaughlin board show you that Ludgin got art has come to tv commercials.

es of film commercials has been aughlin's (to introduce its instant which there is neither live action

nor animation. Instead the series used a technique which might be called symbolism or semi-abstraction. The commercials are being slotted on tv shows in Chicago and other Midwest markets including Milwaukee. Producer is Five Star Productions.

The commercials were conceived and written by Jack Baxter, creative group head, working with John Willmarth, v.p. and creative director, and Hooper White, tv production manager (all of Ludgin).

Both agency and client are enthusiastic about the commercials and sales results. The morning after they first appeared on the air, five agencies called to ask for prints they could show their own creative groups. And sales response was strong.

AGO PAPER HAILED CLIENT'S COURAGE. AD USED LOGO (BELOW) WHICH WAS TAKEOFF ON COMMERCIAL

RLE LUDGIN and Company

1. Typical commercial in series starts with bars. Voice: "Do you have closed mind?"

2. Bars form fence. Voice: "Lots of people bar themselves from best things in life."

3. Bars move off into clump as voice says these people stay off in corner by selves

4. Bars then form into door. Visual devices like this characterize entire film series

5. "May we ask you to open your mind for a moment," says voice as door opens

6. "No, don't close your mind!" says voice as the door slams shut once again

7. Door reopens and letters float out into space to form trademark of the product

8. Four quotes appear. Voice: 'Delightful!' 'So easy to make!' 'Real coffee taste!'

9. Each quote forms word, words form slogan. Music stresses action throughout

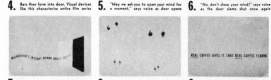

10. Action reverses: Words again become quotes and voice repeats the slogan

11. Quotes form bar, triangle representing scale to weigh lbs. of coffee

12. Scale shows amount of coffee needed for just a few ounces of instant coffee

13. Door theme is used again to familiarize viewers with product package

14. Jar stands in open doorway while voice slowly repeats name of product

15. Door closes quickly. Voice ends commercial: "You'll like it instantly!"

71

DO have fun with your cartoon treatment and use all the tricks of the medium. Let the horse snort, wind up his legs like a pin-wheel and take off like a tornado. And don't overlook sound effects to point up the exaggeration. Your animation director can help on this.

DON'T be prosaic in your cartoon interpretation. Unless
a figure is a trademark, don't be afraid to exaggerate it and
utilize the imaginative possibilities of the medium. Actually,
it is easier to animate an exaggerated cartoon than a true-to-
life animal or person.

LIVE ACTION is the most believable technique in television commercials because it is human, personal experience itself. Seeing is believing.

It permits the viewer to be a part of the action on the screen. *He* can be the person in the situation. It can be *his* hand getting the "feel" of the product, learning to use it. He can more quickly translate this message into *his* life.

Cartoons and puppets are from a make-believe world of fantasy. Stop motion and photo animation are from a make-believe world of camera trickery. Only live action has true reality.

So, wherever this human, personal experience is required for the selling job, live action is indicated.

Live action divides itself into two basic sub-divisions.

1. Narrative style, with the voices off-screen.
2. Dialogue style, with the salesman or actors speaking in direct sound, to each other and to the audience.

Each has specific advantages.

75

LIVE ACTION

ADVANTAGES OF NARRATIVE STYLE

Narrative is slightly less expensive than dialogue and, paradoxically, has a longer life expectancy. Narrative paces faster and concentrates viewer attention with fewer distractions than dialogue.

Rated against all other techniques, narrative live action is best for:

Demonstration, to present a realistic picture of the product in use. This is television salesmanship in action.

Exposition, to quickly set a scene or to introduce by off-screen voice the personality who is to speak.

Human Interest, to show family life, babies, pets. Here is where the viewer's heart can be won.

Appetite Appeal, to show mouth-watering pictures in food films. A perking pot of coffee "translates" in seconds what "still" pictures and words alone can never fully accomplish in minutes.

Many commercials are entirely narrative style with no actors on the screen actually speaking. Despite the contentions of some that the speaker "must be identified" to the audience, the narrative track can be quite anonymous, representing a person in authority or the listener himself, interpreting the scene.

Newsreels and short subjects have long proved the faster pacing and keener interest in the voice-over style. Only key characters speak, and very briefly then. What would a newsreel be like if you had to spend all the time looking at the announcer—or if *all* characters spoke?

ADVANTAGES OF DIALOGUE STYLE

Dialogue has its own special advantages. It is best for:

"Personality" Commercials, directly presented into the camera by a star performer, a special announcer or a company spokesman.

Testimonials, by actual users.

Key Copy Lines, spoken by actors featured in the commercial.

Costs of narrative and dialogue films vary widely, due to casts, settings, props, location trips and many other factors. The cost chart in Chapter 6 suggests an average of $50 per second for narrative films, against $60—or approximately 20% more—for dialogue films.

COMPARATIVE LIFE EXPECTANCY

Narrative films, despite lower costs, normally can be broadcast more times than dialogue films. This is because the salesmen and actors, in dialogue, cannot continue to repeat the same story, over and over, without sounding "stagey" and unbelievable. Every action, every inflection is re-examined by the viewer until he becomes critical of what they do, what they say, and how they say it. If you watch a movie a second time, you know the story and you suddenly become more conscious of *acting performances.*

All-dialogue commercials, with two or more actors carrying the entire action, are generally the most difficult form of television commercial to stage successfully, for this reason. Such films must have a story and it is likely to become less believable with each repetition.

Short testimonial lines and key copy lines, spoken by the actors, do not face this problem. Often such brief dialogue sequences give added impact to an otherwise narrative style commercial.

THE "PERSONALITY" SALESMAN

Television has made much of the "personality" salesman, from the potato-peeler pitchman to the omnipresent Arthur Godfrey. There are many grades in between the two extremes and we need to analyze.

"Arthur Godfrey never reads the commercial," one observer points out, "he delivers it the way you think *you* would,

LIVE ACTION FOR DEMONSTRATION—The Sheaffer Snorkel pen commercials made graphic demonstration of how the "snorkel" reaches out and fills the pen without getting ink on the point. In its first nine months on television it pushed Snorkel sales to first place over competition.

FOR HUMAN INTEREST — Where family scenes, children, pets are to be shown, only live action can achieve an emotional response from the viewer. Cartoon amuses, but live action can touch the heart of the viewer.

FOR APPETITE APPEAL — Nothing replaces live action. Kraft, with live studio commercials, has proved the value of showing huge closeups of food products in preparation and in use. So, open up that food package and show the "promise", ready to eat!

FOR PERSONALITY COMMERICALS—Whether star, sport figure or straight announcer, live action is required to get the personality across. A cartoon of the same person would lose believability. Dialogue live action also is useful for key copy lines.

DO use an "authority" if you have a valid one, fully acceptable and believable to your viewer. The test pilot who cracked 1600 miles an hour is valid for Ralston's *Space Patrol*. It is wise to first check any announcer, actor or authority figure with this question: Is he acceptable and believable to the viewer?

DON'T abuse "medical authority" in commercials. Networks and stations already have clamped down on this type of spot and now require a disclaimer indicating such roles are staged with actors. Does such a film really *sell* the viewer? It seems unlikely. Medical claims must seek another crutch.

making fun of it once in awhile so that you identify yourself with him. He is behaving like you, so he becomes believable."

In live television, Kate Smith, Betty Furness, Art Linkletter and others have proved sales-effective in commercials because they have a vital "personality link" with the viewer. They are natural, believable. Their endorsements carry weight.

Others succeed only in ratio to the size of the circle of viewers who accept them and believe them. The "personality" sales-man must first establish himself as a *human being* to the viewer. He must be a person of known and likeable characteristics. His voice, his looks and his mannerisms must have appeal before he starts to build a loyal audience.

What applies to live television also applies to film in this case. The important thing in putting the "personality" salesman on film is to avoid making the presentation "too perfect". It is the very lack of perfection that often is a clue to the success of the personality.

STARS AND TESTIMONIALS

Often screen stars, sports heroes and other figures of prom-inence are used in commercials with varying success. Again the "per-sonality" factor is the key. The wrong script may submerge the "per-sonality" that the public expects or it may be a case that there is no "personality" to project. The viewer simply rings up "no sale."

It is always a difficult problem to stage dialogue com-mercials with non-professional actors. Self-consciousness and stagi-ness, as well as over-acting, translate all too quickly to the viewer. Wherever possible, keep their lines brief and phrased in their normal conversational manner.

Many professional actors, too, cannot adjust themselves to the television commercial. Fine actors are sometimes poor salesmen. Their experience is entirely in creating *other* characters on the stage or screen—they become typed in the public mind—and it is not easy for them to take off their mask, be themselves . . . and *sell*.

Ask yourself, honestly: Does the viewer believe *they use* the product?

Dialogue live action always is necessary for the testimonial or endorsement to carry conviction. But keep it natural, keep it brief. Keep it believable!

THE 1953 SAG CODE

Actors in television commercials get more money and fewer jobs since the 1953 SAG Code went into effect. The Screen Actors Guild now requires payment to each actor for each broadcast of each film commercial on each network program. This amounts to $70 for the first use and $50 for each reuse—or a maximum of $650 per commercial per 13 weeks' usage. If the same commercial is used in spot markets, the actor must be paid an additional $140 per quarter.

Therefore, an actor who makes 6 commercials in a day— whether he speaks or just appears in a scene—may then receive 6 x $650 plus 6 x $140 each quarter—or a total of $18,960 for the first year's usage for one day's work. This may be more than the writer's total budget for the 6 films.

Off-screen voices and singers receive smaller payments and the scale drops for regional and local usage, whether program or spot. No attempt will be made here to go into the many ramifications of the SAG Code, but it is vital that the creative writer carefully study these scales in order that budget limitations can be observed.[1]

Obviously, only essential actors should be used. Often "names", stars and prominent endorsements can be obtained for no more than these new scale costs.

WEIGH THE FACTORS CAREFULLY

There has been a tendency to switch much former live action to cartoon as a result of the SAG Code. This is not always wise, as you may thereby sacrifice selling impact.

[1] For further information on the SAG Code and its effect on costs see *The Handbook of TV and Film Technique* by Charles W. Curran, published 1953 by Visual Arts Books — Farrar, Straus and Young, New York.

DO concentrate on small casts and close-ups. It is generally necessary for a person to be on the screen for some seconds before the viewer decides whether he "likes him or not". Time devoted to fewer persons permits the screen personality to get across better. Once the scene has been established, try to stay with close-ups.

DON'T use too many people in your cast—under the SAG
code. Not only is it expensive, but it is also difficult for a
large group to translate to the viewer in terms of "personality" unless successive close-ups follow. Wherever possible,
stick with one or two, so that they have time to ingratiate
themselves with the audience.

DO win confidence with informality. For an announcer or
personality to sell the viewer he must first "make friends"
or prove common interest. This second film with Rupert
Hughes accomplished this more quickly through informality. Note that even the camera angle and broken pattern
of the background help.

DON'T build a barrier for your "straight pitch" personality. Here the setting is too straight and formal; a desk stands between the voice and the viewer. Psychologically, most people have had a bad experience with someone "across a desk" and this situation does not win confidence. This particular film was shot two ways.

PROCESS BACKGROUNDS — Certain exterior settings are best achieved with the use of process backgrounds. Cameramen first shoot the setting on location, then in the studio this background is rear projected on a large screen, with the actors and certain relevant props in the foreground. Much used in Hollywood movies, this method is fairly expensive for the average commercial, yet it is cheaper than actually taking cast and crew to remote locations.

BACKDROPS —: For a difficult shot of steel girders, for instance, the simplest production procedure is to build girders of wood and use a sky backdrop which is kept in soft focus. Such settings still can be quite expensive, and it is vital that a writer have knowledge of production methods and costs before indicating such scenes in a script. This same scene, for instance, would be less expensive if staged in a locker room, against a brick wall, or against the sky backdrop only.

GOING ON LOCATION: If the script calls for a large view of a supermarket, it can be costly. The producer is forced to make a night location trip with cast and crew at premium rates or go to even greater expense to build such a large set in a studio. Generally, such scenes are better handled in close shots, more readily staged in a studio, and are then representative in the viewer's mind of *any* supermarket rather than the *one* particular supermarket.

BUILDING LARGE SETS: It is not normally feasible to stage dialogue live action on locations such as service stations, due to extraneous noises always present. The building of such a studio set costs $3000 and up and is justified only if there are a great number of scenes and a number of commercials to be shot simultaneously, thereby amortizing the cost. Good scripting must weigh such cost factors in advance.

91

Review the advantages of live action. You can still demonstrate, because you can use closeups of the product and show human hands in action—as long as the actor's face does not appear.

You can still have coffee perking, foods steaming hot, and many other scenes for appetite appeal. However, adult "reaction shots" are costly now. Less often does father drool over the product and wink into the camera and the passing of this phase of the commercial is probably the finest thing that could have happened to the industry! The viewer was fairly fed up with the parade of beaming, smirking, winking faces that had been greeting him every time he turned on his set.

The SAG Code has been a hard blow to a growing industry, but in the long run it may effect a great good. It has brought about more intelligent planning and it has stopped the overuse of poor commercials.

But it must never be used as an excuse for omitting live action when live action is essential to the advertising job.

Live action remains the most useful technique in television commercials because it is live, because it is real, because it is the common denominator of experience that can reach out and shake hands with the viewer.

CHAPTER 9

Stop Motion:

Mechanical Ingenuity

STOP MOTION is a technique that has always intrigued the advertising man far more than it has the viewer. Because it is intricate to produce, it is a common error to get so carried away with the mechanics of the technique that the basic advertising job is forgotten.

Lucky Strike's "marching cigarette" commercials, which were patterned after the Muratti cigarette films produced in Europe in the 1930's, first called attention to the possibilities of the technique in Television, U. S. A.

Here was a way to make inanimate objects come to life! Eureka!

But it was not as simple as that. Even though the viewer was charmed and delighted in seeing the Lucky Strike films again and again, it became necessary for Luckies to go to brand-battle commercials to keep up with the competition.

Nonetheless, these were great films from a technical as well as an audience standpoint and served a very important function in stimulating advertisers, producers and viewers to want better television commercials.

Some of the Lucky Strike films cost more than $7,500 per minute, which gives some idea of the technical man-hours and craftsmanship involved.

FRAME-BY-FRAME EXPOSURE

Like the cartoon, this technique of stop motion works on one frame of film—1/24th of a second—at a time. The product is set up and photographed for the first single frame, then moved to its next carefully planned position, photographed again, and so on. The result is that 24 successive single photographs, when projected on the screen in one second's time, give the illusion of a definitely fluid movement.

Imagine the planning and skill involved in moving *each* of the cigarettes to *each* of the successive positions required. Sixty seconds is 1,440 single set-ups, 1,440 single photographs!

Scotch Brand Tape followed Lucky Strike with a more practical commercial. Again a march was called for and the product marched into every room in the house. At this point in the commericals, live action inserts gave a believable demonstration of uses.

DARING YOUNG PANCAKES

Still more practical was the use of stop motion made by Pillsbury Pancake Mix. The copy theme was "Lighter pancakes are here!" and the visual selling was to be done by having the pancakes tossed in the air and lightly, very slowly, float over and down to the serving plate.

To accomplish this, pancakes were cooked over aluminum discs (to hold the shape, yet permit bending where the effect of motion required it); then, by a system of hidden armatures, the pancakes were suspended in mid-air step-by-step, photograph-by-photograph, as they travelled the slow arc from griddle to plate.

After the props were completed, the mechanics set up and the master plan prepared, it still required more than 16 camera hours to photograph this one :20 spot!

Pillsbury's "floating pancakes" is an example of creative imagination developing an advertising idea, "Lighter pancakes are here!" This film ran more than a hundred times on the Arthur Godfrey show.

ADVANTAGES OF THE TECHNIQUE

Stop motion has three advantages, the first shared with cartoon, the last shared with live action. Stop motion is best for:

Personalizing of the Product, such as the marching cigarettes. The product can be made to dance, fly, zoom or take itself apart and put itself together again.

Mechanical Action, such as fitting of parts of a motor, or the addition of attachments to an appliance.

Demonstration, without human hands. The refrigerator can magically fill with shelf after shelf of foods. The doors of a range can mysteriously open and a luscious cake slide out.

Industrial films have long used stop motion to show mechanical action. Similar use for television commercials is more rare, simply because good selling is more concerned with consumer benefits than the mechanics of manufacture. Pillsbury's use is unusual in that it actually excited an emotional appeal.

Stop motion vies with cartoon in personalizing the product. In cartoon, it is the practice to "put a face" on the product. In stop motion, it is the practice to show the product exactly as it is.

FIRST, ASK TWO QUESTIONS

Stop motion vies with live action on demonstration and a careful decision needs to be made in the choice of technique. Ask yourself:

Which will demonstrate more effectively?

DO use stop motion to arrest attention and excite interest
in features of the product. Here the special foil inner-wrap
bag jumps out of the Sugar Pops box, dances with "energy"
and then fills the bowl, all in stop motion. Live action follows for appetite appeal.

DON'T use stop motion without subsequent live action demonstration to follow it. It is intriguing to have the oven doors open and food mysteriously slide out in stop motion, but the viewer's mind personalizes it more when a woman follows up with live action demonstration.

DO use stop motion where it can inexpensively demonstrate ideas more graphically than other techniques. Here, a closing scene was needed to associate Chee-Wees with beer, coke, milk and cocktails. Each popped in, in rapid succession.

DON'T attempt to do intricate stop motion films unless you know the high costs involved. This scene is from a Muratti cigarette theater film made in Germany in 1933 by Oskar Fischinger. Lucky Strike introduced the idea in this country for TV. Cost per film: $7,500!

Which will sell more convincingly?

In other words, is it better to have that cake mysteriously slide out of the opened oven door or is it better to have a housewife actually take it out herself and hold it for her family—and the viewer to see and experience?

A decision on this point needs to be made. Generally it is solved by following up the interest-getting stop motion with a more natural, a more believable live action scene.

In the case of Kellogg's Sugar Corn Pops, the product excited opening interest with a Western dance in a miniature setting, followed by live action scenes of kids in Western atmosphere enjoying cereal.

Stop motion costs an average of $40 per second when it is a single object doing a fairly simple motion. More objects and more complex routines increase the cost, as in the case of Lucky Strike. Where special models must be constructed, as in the case of Pillsbury, additional charges are required.

Just remember never to get so intrigued with the fascinating mechanics of the stop motion technique that you forget to do your basic advertising job.

CHAPTER 10

Puppets:

Some Are "Dolls"

THERE ARE three types of puppets for television commercials: string puppets, hand puppets and frame-by-frame or stop motion puppets made in the George Pal method.

String puppets, or marionettes, and hand puppets both require the continuity of a regular program to build viewer interest.

Howdy Doody represents a good example of the string puppet, built through skillful programming into a "personality." This is the vital factor that makes "Howdy" a successful commercial salesman. It is almost impossible to create a new puppet and have it do a selling job before it is built into such a "personality" status.

This is likewise true of hand puppets. *Kukla, Fran and Ollie* became a successful vehicle only because Burr Tillstrom's clever creations became personalities of known value, with all the characteristics and idiosyncrasies of human beings.

Time for Beany is another example of good program development of a hand puppet into the realm of "personality" commercial possibilities.

BUT MANY FAILURES

In spite of these three unusual winning examples there are dozens of failures in the puppet field, from a commercial standpoint. Much of the argument for the use of a "personality" in live action dialogue commercials, as outlined a couple of chapters back, can be directly applied here.

Various attempts have been made to bring to life trademark characters in hand or string puppets, but most of these have failed in the television commercial field. The creation and manipulation of such characters is simply too limited to achieve best results.

Quite another thing is the frame-by-frame "dolls" where expression, animation and characterization can be achieved without the limitation of strings and one-expression faces.

George Pal created this frame-by-frame technique in Amsterdam and used it successfully in many European theater film commercials before coming to this country to produce the erstwhile Paramount *Puppetoons*. Puppets, of course, always have been far more successful as entertainment in Europe than in America.

SIMILARITY TO CARTOON

The technique borrows from two other fields, cartoon and stop motion. The dolls have not a single face but actually dozens, each carefully modeled in third dimension to show every step of changing expression.

Miniature or scale settings are built and the frame-by-frame dolls operate therein by a system of intricate registration. Photography is by stop motion, one frame at a time. For each 1/24 of a second's action, the doll's body is moved and the head *changed* to another head that befits the required move in expression (even as a new drawing is made for a cartoon sequence).

This is photographed, and the process continues, as it would with the Lucky Strike cigarettes, except now a change of facial expression and body action is possible.

The making of the dolls is extremely tedious, but once

completed, they have an advantage over cartoon in that they can be used again and again in different settings, with different sequences of action.

ADVANTAGES OF TECHNIQUE

There are two primary advantages of puppets as a technique and both of these vie with cartoon. Puppets are best for:

Trademark Characters, provided the trademark has not already been established as a cartoon figure in other media.

Singing Jingles, where dimensional effects are desired. Characters and sets can be staged as "miniature musical comedies."

Heinz "57" Varieties used frame-by-frame puppets to bring their Aristocrat Tomato trademark character to life. Scores of heads were produced, each identical in form but with varying expressions to cover the necessities of the first series of soup commercials.

Given a hearty voice in the pre-recorded sound track, the characters came to life with authority. However, only about one-fourth of the commercial time was given to the puppet; live action carried the bulk of the sales story.

Peter Paul Candy also used this technique as a "miniature musical comedy." The "king" bar sang and told his story, surrounded by cocoanut trees and chocolate, with a chorus of other Peter Paul bars.

Goebel Beer also has used the technique successfully, with "Brewster, the Goebel Rooster", strutting, singing and dancing. The Goebel films have been produced in Holland by Joop Geesink, via Transfilm. Geesink makes his dolls of plastic, so movable heads are not required, but a stop-motion camera technique is required to shoot the production frame-by-frame.

Maurice Seidermann, make-up expert who developed the plastic "face" for motion picture makeup, has done considerable work in a similar type of puppet. The same type of flexible plastic face that aged Orson Welles in "Citizen Kane" is adapted by Seidermann to the puppets of "Time for Beany" and puppet commercial use.

103

NO STRINGS ON HIM! "Mr. Aristocrat Tomato", the Heinz trademark character, was created for the George Pal frame-by-frame puppet technique. He "loses his head" 24 times per second, a new head with a new expression (and a change in body movement) being photographed in successive stop motion exposures. Cost of the original "dolls" is high, but can be amortized in a continuing series of films comparable with cartoon cost. Relative effectiveness of puppets vs. cartoon is always a debatable point.

Bob Baker and others have done notable work in the field of stringless puppets, as well.

PUPPETS VS. CARTOON

By and large, this technique is better than cartoon for any trademark character that has a "dimensional" tone quality, rather than the single-plane quality of a sketch drawing. In other words, if your trademark character now looks like a cartoon in other media, keep it in the cartoon technique for television.

JOOP GEESINK DOLL! "Brewster, the Goebel Rooster" differs from the Heinz Aristocrat Tomato in that he is a flexible puppet, completely movable. No separate heads are needed, the plastic being readily manipulated into changing expressions. Joop Geesink of Holland creates these 8″ dolls, filmed exclusively for Transfilm in this country. Both Geesink and Pal-type dolls are shot in stop-motion, 1/24th of a second per successive movement, and can achieve perfect talking, singing and dancing effects.

The frame-by-frame doll technique is fairly expensive to start. The various heads and bodies may run from $2,000 to $5,000 for creation, after which production costs drop to as low as $25 per second, depending on the number of "units" or characters and the complexity of the movement.

String puppets and hand puppets are much less costly, both in creation and production, and also are comparatively less effective.

The important question to ask on the possible use of a puppet is simply: "Is it a personality?" Or can it be developed into a "personality" without too much experimentation and expense?

Speedy Alka-Seltzer is a George Pal type of puppet, originated by Five Star Productions. He can cough, sneeze, sing and do many tricks through the stop-motion use of a series of replaceable heads.

This plastic-type puppet, operated mechanically by remote control, was developed by Maurice Seidermann, Hollywood makeup expert. It operates either in continuous motion or in stop-motion photography.

CHAPTER 11

Photo Animation:

The Budget Saver

PHOTO ANIMATION is the low budget technique that can sometimes give the illusion of more expensive live action or stop motion.

It is photographed on a flat bed camera stand, like the cartoon, using stills, sketches and titles and it depends largely on the camera for optical tricks and movement.

Called "Fotan" by some producers, this is the technique that can achieve effects valuable beyond actual costs. It is the "budget balancer" of the script writer. It is a rare script which cannot use some of it—but there is practically no script that can use all of it. Photo animation needs to be blended with other techniques.

Titles, logos and signatures, where not superimposed over live action, are easily handled in photo animation. Zooming boxes, spinning bottles, flashing effects all are Fotan's stock-in-trade.

PHOTO ANIMATION

ADVANTAGES OF PHOTO ANIMATION

The advantages of photo animation indicate it is best for:

Special Announcements, similar to movie theater trailers which are largely titles and tricks.

Retouching Products, such as appliances of glass and bright chrome. After retouching, the still photographs are then reproduced on motion picture film.

"Catalog" of Products, where a complete line of related items or related adaptations can be shown. Here photo animation can strip the scene to essentials and present many items, rapidly, in sequence.

Signatures, such as end most commercials. The package, the logo, the slogan can readily be presented to best advantage in this technique, inexpensively.

FOTAN WORKS FOR WORK CLOTHES

In the case of Dickies' Work Clothes, a sequence called for demonstration of the fact that the fabric was sanforized and would not shrink in washing. Photo animation was used to illustrate.

First, eight still photographs were made of the garment in the various stages of being dipped into a tub of water. The photographs were then retouched and mounted in an animation cycle sequence.

A wash-tub and a simple cycle of animated soap bubbles were drawn and finally a title "Sanforized" was made for superimposure.

On the screen, the viewer saw the work clothes dip themselves into the tub again and again, while the soap bubbles flew and "Sanforized" appeared. Cost: negligible. Effect: most graphic.

IT BORROWS TRICKS FROM ANIMATION

Good photo animation requires the services of a writer or director who knows all the tricks of limited animation. If he knows

108

Photo Animation permits retouching of still photographs to show cut-aways. By superimposing photos on separate cels, these then are rephotographed on motion picture film with dissolves or other optical transitions made right in the camera.

Closing signatures can be done inexpensively in photo animation. Hotpoint used successive pop-ons of sketched hands (not animated) and title lettering to sync with: "Point — point — to Hotpoint! Look to Hotpoint for the Finest First!"

PHOTO ANIMATION — Knapp-Monarch used inexpensive Photo Animation to show the operation of the K-M Liquidizer. Ice cubes (photographic) were moved by single-frame exposure to the top of the glass, then whirled rapidly downward. Meanwhile, a photograph of crushed ice replaced the previous one, came out of the whirl, and moved off screen at lower right. Tomatoes to tomato juice and cabbage to cole slaw were handled the same way, in fast succession, demonstrating the "idea" of the Liquidizer without showing all the messy details. It was more graphic than Live Action.

CATALOG OF PRODUCTS — Photo animation also is excellent where a number of different products must be shown on the screen. In this scene retouched photos were utilized, along with cartoon. Each product popped on the screen, in succession, as the jingle detailed its merits. The same photos were used for close-ups later in the film.

his craft, he can make two still photographs of a person dissolve and get the effect of a smile.

The opening title of the Tide "Red" Skelton show was first done in photo animation. Boxes popped on, the letters of "T-I-D-E" appeared and Skelton did a grimace—a highly intriguing use of an inexpensive technique.

To make a box zoom up to full screen in photo animation, a series of photographic prints are made in varying sizes from infinity to full screen size. These are then mounted in sequence and photographed frame-by-frame as they get larger and larger. Retouching may be done, titles superimposed, backgrounds changed to fit.

Optical "wipes" (trick visual devices between scenes which "wipe" away the old picture and "wipe" on a new) may be added in photography at a fraction of the cost of laboratory opticals and special effects. Dissolves or cross-fades between scenes and camera movement of all types are relatively inexpensive.

HOW TO MAKE TOMATO JUICE

Knapp-Monarch Appliances used a photo animation sequence to symbolize how their Liquidizer would make tomatoes into tomato juice, cabbages into cole slaw, ice cubes into crushed ice.

The appliance (a retouched photo) dominated the scene in the center, and at the top left still photographs of a tomato, a cabbage and a bowl of ice cubes moved in procession to the center and dissolved out as it whirled down.

Meanwhile, dissolving in at the center of the appliance and heading camera right were the moving photographs of the completed dishes.

Photo animation costs an average of $20 per second, with most of this being budgeted for the skillful animation director.

Never expect photo animation to do the trick of a special effects department. For what it is, it is fine: a craftsman's tool to do a good job, occasionally a spectacular job, at low cost. It can help to balance your aching budget.

CHAPTER 12

Working To A Budget:

Blending Techniques

NOW THAT we have pin-pointed the advantages of each of the five production techniques and we know the average cost of each, we are ready to devise the commercial to a specific budget.

Before the actual script is written, it is well to decide which technique will do the best job for the money to be spent.

Cartoon and live action are the two techniques most often joined in the same commercial, but it is also feasible to use any other two or three in combination. And photo animation always stands ready to help balance the budget.

Cartoon costs an average of $80 a second. Live action, narrative style, costs an average of $50 a second. Photo animation costs an average of only $20 a second.

Why not blend them—if we get the advantages we want—and work to a budget?

CASE HISTORY OF AN ANALYSIS

Here is an example of how the charts shown in earlier chapters, "Basic Sales Objectives," "Average Cost" and "Advantages" were used in the creation of the S.O.S. "Magic Bunny" series of commercials for NBC *Show of Shows*. The development of a single 1:00 commercial for use in an hour-and-a-half variety show offered many problems.

First, analysis aimed the series in the field of primary selling toward these three purposes: 1) winning new customers, 2) holding repeat customers and 3) increasing use per capita. Other aims, for later consideration, were "new uses" and institutional.

Step-by-step, the analysis considered production techniques:

S.O.S. COMMERCIALS FOR "SHOW OF SHOWS"
Possible Production Techniques:

1. ANIMATED CARTOON—Best for gaining interest, because the cartoon is the universal medium of entertainment. Best for delineating any trademark character or a new character representative of the qualities of the product.

    For S.O.S.—on *Show of Shows,* cartoon would be highly desirable. If we can create a cartoon character representative of the "magic" and speed of S.O.S., it will serve a valuable double purpose. Also, with cartoon, the films can be repeated many times.

2. STOP-MOTION—Best for bringing inanimate objects to life.

    For S.O.S.—Not too good, since the box and pads gain little interest by movement. The entire demonstration could be done in stop-motion "magic", but we seriously question whether the housewife will accept this as a practical demonstration.

3. DIALOGUE LIVE ACTION—Best for the testimonial type of commercial or "personality" announcer.

> For S.O.S. — We advise against an "announcer pitch" as this is overdone and will not hold a maximum number of viewers between the acts of the show. However, dialogue sequence might be useful in testimonials of housewives speaking from experience.

3B. NARRATIVE LIVE ACTION—Best for demonstration or any expositional type of film.

> For S.O.S.—The only technique for best demonstrating its working qualities, with the action quickly taking place while the narrative voice describes and *sells*.

4. PUPPETS—Best for trademark characters and singing jingles.

> For S.O.S.—Not as flexible as cartoon for this sponsor.

5. PHOTO ANIMATION—Best low-budget method of presenting inanimate objects or a "catalog" of several products.

> For S.O.S.—Not useful. We have only one product to sell—not several. We must sell it in keeping with the caliber of the show.

Out of this analysis, which shows the advantages of using cartoon to gain opening interest, then live action to demonstrate, came the creation of the S.O.S. "Magic Bunny."

WHAT TO REPEAT IN A SERIES

It is often wise to repeat a basic sales point, graphically done, in identical fashion in every film in the series. Many sponsors still try to get "a little different camera angle" or rephrase the wording on such sequences, but this defeats the repetitive series impact you should achieve in driving home a basic sales point.

When the sales job can be done in one *right* way in :40,

115

you need only to hook on a variety of :20 openings to have a series. Pabst Blue Ribbon, and Tea Council and many others have used this formula successfully. It increases cumulative impact and also can save production cost.

Never be afraid to repeat any good scene in identical fashion in every film in the series. A demonstration sequence becomes more familiar to the viewer with each showing until he actually *experiences* using the product.

Do not try to repeat scenes with people's faces. These get tiresome and here the viewer expects variety. What's more: you have to pay for each use of a person's face in each commercial under the SAG code. The fact that it is an identical scene makes no difference in these talent payments.

Do not try to repeat "examples," such as a recipe. It is wiser to shoot as many versions as you have films.

Do not repeat identical scenes at the opening of a film, because here you are trying to gain viewer interest. Win them first, then sell them.

OPENING INTEREST

Any survey of the effectiveness of a television commercial that fails to consider opening viewer interest, does not do a complete job. Whether you use cartoon, live action or other technique at the start does not matter, as long as you do win interest and attention.

The opening must be relevant, of course. It must relate to the product story you are to tell and it must relate to the viewer, personally.

The first five seconds often are the most vital because here your audience is won or lost. Viewers can leave the television room or they may *mentally* turn off the set and turn on the conversation.

Cartoon is ideal for opening interest, because it says "fun!" to the viewer. In live action, a personality, babies, or family life can excite interest. In stop motion, commercials such as the Scotch Tape march and the Pillsbury floating pancakes have quick fascination.

Always, however, the opening must be carefully linked to

the story that follows. Don't use a baby and say "It's new!" to open a commercial on a new fishing rod. Both may be new, but the two ideas actually conflict. Make it relevant to mood, product and story.

TRANSITIONS BETWEEN TECHNIQUES ARE EASY

There is no problem in going from cartoon to live action if the chain-of-images is logical in development. The cartoon "Magic Bunny" can start the live action demonstration. The live action baby can logically carry the mind to a cartoon milk drop. The live action housewife can lead into the stop motion demonstration of the washing machine.

Often straight cuts can be made between sequences. At other times, a simple dissolve bridges the transition.

Folger's Coffee successfully used the cartoon jingle of the "Four Happy Cups." The film opened with a quartet singing, then as each cup sang his solo of accomplishments, the camera merely panned over and cut to a live action scene. Dad's cup, Mother's cup, the demitasse cup and the restaurant mug each sang in cartoon before cutting to appetizing live action scenes. A total of 10 direct cuts were made between cartoon and live action in this minute film—yet the viewer was unaware of a change of techniques because each step was logical.

Use the technique that tells each phase of your story best. Never be afraid to mix and blend. Check back to the advantages and uses, keep your chain-of-images smooth and make the parts relevant to the overall selling job. It is easier than it sounds.

You can use brick, cement, glass and wood to build a house. The viewer doesn't look at it in terms of individual materials —he views it as a home for himself. He rejects it if it is too ornamental or non-functional. He expects to see glass in the windows (he wants to know what's going on!) but if you build an all-glass house, he's liable to throw stones at it.

DO mix cartoon and live if *only the cartoon moves*. Then the "live" part can be a still photograph, such as this background for the S.O.S. "Magic Bunny", and the cost is no higher than normal cartoon animation.

DON'T mix live action and cartoon in the same scene *if* the live action *moves*. It can be done but usually requires an expensive technical process. Always consult an expert before planning such tricky scenes in TV commercials.

DO back up the cartoon idea with live action "example". The two techniques can be readily intercut (without opticals) when the subject matter is closely related. The Folger film used 5 cartoon scenes with 4 live action scenes directly intercut.

DON'T expect cartoon to do your complete selling job. Cartoons are excellent to win interest, but they need to be backed with live action for appetite appeal and demonstration. This Folger film cut to each of the "4 Happy Cups" in live action.

There's a nostalgic quality to the "good old days" but it often looks only "corny" when staged in live action. Armour's Miss Wisconsin Cheese wanted to capture the quality idea expressed by the "good old days" yet show how modern packaging has improved the product. Cartoon was used for the opening, then live action followed. Incidentally, this one opening scene would have cost ten times as much in live action.

Sentiment, the good wishes of the holiday season, is better done in live action — but is always difficult and requires good taste in writing, acting and direction. Cartoon would never have done this scene with equivalent human interest and validity, so live action was the only choice. By amortizing set costs in a series of 18 films, the final production budget was actually less than cartoon.

CHAPTER 13

The Sound Track:

The Singing Jingle

SOUND CAN soothe the mind, terrorize the mind, stimulate the mind.

In television commercials, sound can work hand-in-hand with the picture to penetrate the mind more deeply, more convincingly.

Consider your tools:

1. Sound effects
2. Announcer voices
3. Actor voices
4. Trick voices of cartoon
5. Singing jingles
6. Rhythm chants

The relative values of sight and sound vary with each commercial.

Station break spots require a heavier emphasis on sound, because often you must catch your viewer by ear only as he wanders from the set.

Jingles and chants, too, rely more heavily on sound.

THE SOUND TRACK

SOUND AND IMAGINATION

Radio has long proved that sound can open the doors of imagination. In fact, radio here has an advantage over television.

The whistle of a train, the bark of a dog, the cry of a baby all stir subconscious meanings in the mind of the viewer, but when these things are actually pictured on the screen, they limit the imagination to *one specific*. This may not be the particular train or dog or baby that radio would have conjured up from the viewer's experiences —and a vital link with the subconscious is missed.

Television often is wise to play these sound effects against the pictured reaction of a person's face, so that imagination can have a freer rein. Cartoon picturization also is broad enough to allow full play of imagination.

SOUND EFFECTS

Sound effects get attention. Whenever relevant, they are excellent to open a commercial.

Many such devices are hackneyed, but consider the use of a telephone bell, a rifle shot, an ambulance siren, a foghorn, a fight gong, a door chime and all the standbys of radio. On :10 and :20 station break spots they are especially useful. But always they must be an integral part of your story.

Sound effects can be the soul of imagination. They stir up pictures in the mind.

THE NEXT VOICE YOU HEAR

Voices have been discussed in the chapter on live action, but there is more to be said concerning the quality and character of voices.

Announcers and actors should be selected first of all for authority and believability. The voice must not be too glib, too affected, too patronizing. And the voice must "fit the face" whenever used on camera.

Competence is more important than "name value" in select-

126

ing an announcer for off-screen voice. Many announcers who are unknown nationally are extremely competent in specializing in the needs of appetite appeal, romantic, "hard sell" and prestige types of copy.

Women? Not so good. Women are rarely effective in selling products to men and, psychologists say, do not inspire too much confidence in other women. Kate Smith and Betty Furness are exceptions and unless a woman can develop similar authority and "personality" she is a poor risk as a TV commercial announcer.

OFF THE NORMAL

The voice that will make the deepest impression is not one that lulls to sleep. It must penetrate the mind with conviction.

The voice must have character. It must be clearly understood through the three or four reproductions essential to film recording and broadcast.

It should stand out from the rest of television programming sufficiently to excite viewer interest. Often, a mild distortion of the voice in the final dubbing of television commercials aids in achieving this effect.

But warmth and believability must never be sacrificed. It should be different from normal, but not *too* different.

In cartoons, of course, the off-the-norm voice is the secret of success. One remembers "Donald Duck," "Bugs Bunny" or "Porky Pig" as much for voice as anything else. It is the voice that children imitate.

There is much room for improvement in the casting, coaching and recording of voices for the television commercial.

THE SINGING JINGLE

Words set to music live longer.

You can remember a song while you forget a speech. The New York Post surveyed the public and found 4 out of 5 approve singing commercials.

Pepsi-Cola gets credit for the radio jingle trend, "Chiquita

Banana" for the theater ad-film trend, and BVD for the television trend—although these were by no means first in their fields.

Rhythm patterns make learning easy. Most people still remember how many days in a month by a simple rhyme "Thirty days hath September . . ." It works for education, it works for advertising—because good advertising is, as always, a form of education.

But the singing jingle cannot solve every problem.

WHERE JINGLES FAIL

Most singing commercials neglect to do the necessary basic advertising job. They are from the world of fun—like the cartoon— and rarely do a complete selling job in themselves.

For "impulse" items such as soft drinks and cigarettes where a purchase may be made without weighing the facts—singing jingles can sway a certain segment of the market. But they cannot sell refrigerators and automobiles unless backed with some good strong reason-why straight sell.

The results with any jingle cannot be guaranteed. It is a hazardous business at best. It combines creative writing, creative musicianship—and creative advertising. Any one of the three is unpredictable enough!

The use of public domain melodies is rarely recommended. Perhaps it is true that a song that lives half a century has to be good —but it is also true that this song may have conflicting connotations for the listener. The woman who feels romantic about *You Tell Me Your Dream* won't feel kindly toward the toothpaste that borrows it for a singing commercial.

Also against public domain music is the fact that the melody cannot be copyrighted and the sponsor has nothing exclusive but a set of lyrics in borrowed pants. His competition or any other advertiser can use the identical music.

WHERE JINGLES SUCCEED

Original music as well as words are far better. True, they

may "borrow" from public domain music—but they can be completely retailored to the specific job.

Most successful commercials are synonymous with "happy advice":

"Be Happy . . . Go Lucky!"

"Cleans your Breath as it Cleans Your Teeth!"

"Tide gets clothes cleaner than any soap!"

The key copy advice—and the name of the product—need to be the part that comes to mind when the tune is recalled.

When the jingle is properly constructed, this key advertising material then is "re-broadcast" as children and adults pick it up and sing it. It is these "extra broadcasts" in the mind and in the home that is the cheapest television "time" you can buy.

But it is important that the viewer not only *know* the words, but *understand* them. That is why the jingle frequently must be backed up with copy that explains and gives the reason why.

To know the words of "Ajax, the foaming cleanser" is not enough. The woman must understand "foaming" not as just two notes in a happy musical phrase, but as an actual descriptive action. She must visualize Ajax foaming in her own sink as it "washes dirt right down the drain." At the same time, the commercial must sufficiently expose her to the package so that, when she sees it in the store, all these personal interpretations come back to her . . . and she will buy!

BUILDING A JINGLE

There are no yardsticks for the construction of a jingle. But these points may be helpful:
1. Write the words first. Try and see how many ways the key copy lines can go in meter.
2. Work to feature the name of the product *and* the key copy advice in the top musical phrase of the jingle, where it will be most remembered.

3. Try to stay in the idiom of the day. If you can tie a popular expression to your product you have gained an advantage. ("What'll you have?")

4. Keep emotional appeal high. Try to fit into the viewer's experience. Most jingles are fun—be bright, like a bird in a tree, if you want passers-by to look and listen.

5. Repeat and repeat and repeat. Keep it short and keep it basic. Add spoken lines, straight announcing to complete your sales story.

6. The music is a job for an expert. He'll probably "borrow"—but at least he'll know what he is stealing from.

7. The music isn't good unless you can recognize it without the words—and like it!

8. Give it a test campaign to prove it. No one can be certain you have a "hit tune" until a certain amount of repetition proves acceptance.

There is always a question to be asked. It should be asked first, but no one will listen to it then. It is: Are you really sure you need a jingle?

Just because competition has clicked with a jingle, don't try to ride a scooter in the parade. A jingle has no guarantee of popularity and success—and even its success is no guarantee of sales.

THE RHYTHM CHANT

Television has developed a cousin of the jingle which has been called the "rhythm chant." It is more spoken than sung, it has more advertising than melody and it repeats to a point just short of irritation.

The name, slogan or key copy advice is repeated again and again. It can become hypnotic in its penetration, if judiciously used.

The secret is simple, easy-rhyming copy in couplets, each followed by a straight line and sound effect or repetitive device. It has the childish charm of Calypso—but does a very grownup selling job.

Kellogg's Sugar Corn Pops, Tappan Range and others have used the "rhythm chant" effectively, but one of the most successful series has been made by Soil-Off, a household cleaner, with this copy:

The Soil-Off Chant

ANNCR:	Here's a happy lady who's learned the trick Of cleaning house so easy and quick
CHARACTER:	Off with the soil with Soil-Off—
SOUND:	WASHAWAY—WASHAWAY— WHISH!
ANNCR: WOMAN:	To clean that paint, here's welcome news: Just pour from the bottle—it's ready to use!
CHARACTER:	Off with the soil with Soil-Off—
SOUND:	WASHAWAY—WASHAWAY— WHISH!
ANNCR: WOMAN:	No messy rags—no drippy pails— It's ready mixed—it never fails!
CHARACTER:	Off with the soil with Soil-Off—
SOUND:	WASHAWAY—WASHAWAY— WHISH!
ANNCR: WOMAN:	Let Soil-Off clean your bathroom, too— And kitchen walls? They look like new!
CHARACTER:	Off with the soil with Soil-Off—
SOUND:	WASHAWAY—WASHAWAY— WHISH!
ANNCR: WOMAN: ANNCR:	So keep paint clean this easy way— (SYNC) "Why, it's easy as dusting!" —Try it today!
CHARACTER:	Off with the soil with Soil-Off—
ANNCR:	Buy it . . . and try it . . . today!

131

DO use music with cartoon jingles wherever possible. AFM music rates now are lower than SAG voice rates so that it is wiser to back a vocal soloist with an orchestra than with a quartet. Musicians, unlike actors, get no re-payments.

DON'T use jingle singers "on camera" unless you are prepared to pay, generally, twice as much as you would for the same jingle with off-screen voices. This curious feature of the SAG code has increased the use of cartoon for jingles.

DO be certain any "trademark characters" you create are completely appropriate to your product. Here, for the 7-Eleven groceries, TV created a Rooster to open up at 7 a. m., an Owl to close up at 11 p. m. The resultant jingle ran over 4,800 times!

DON'T overlook the cartoon jingling possibilities of any "trademark characters" now in use. If the characters appear on the package, so much the better, because they will then build identification in the stores as a result of their TV appearance.

DO give the woman announcer a "prop", if possible, to open her commercial. Woman talk that way, for one thing, and a "prop" increases opening interest in the commercial and diverts attention from her own personality until she can establish herself and win her audience.

DON'T let your woman announcer be too aggressive. She
will antagonize all men, and many women. She must, however, speak with authority, either from experience or special knowledge of the product. A woman announcer is always a hazardous risk and few can please all viewers.

STATION-BREAK TV spots pack plenty of power. They can be the electronic rifle bullets of advertising, hitting specific markets with precision.

The :10 Station Identification (called "ID") spot is more a "reminder" type of advertising, but it can have movement and high impact.

Here are three of the advantages of the :10 ID and the :20 over the minute commercials.

1. *Sustained Impact.* Being shorter, they can sustain a stronger sales pitch than the 1:00.
2. *Longer Life.* They can stand more repetition than films of greater length.
3. *Easier Scheduling.* More intense coverage can be obtained on more stations, as local sales problems demand.

Both the :10 ID and the :20 need the graphic, simple, clear-cut selling idea expressed with visual certainty.

The video is vital, since it must stick in the mind long after the clock hand has passed the station break. But the audio is vital, too. Sound track alone must catch the viewer who has strayed from the room but still *hears* his television set.

STATION-BREAK SPOTS

SPECIFICATIONS:

Most :10 IDs have :07 of sound track, to meet specifications of network stations, although some individual TV stations restrict this to :06 and others permit :07½ or :08.

The picture runs a full :10, the additional time being allowed for the station to identify its call letters and channel number, audio-wise.

It is well to double-check each station in advance of production for specific requirements.

The important difference in the :10 ID is the general requirement that the upper right 25% of the screen carry visually the individual station's call letters and channel number. This, of course, means that specific prints must be produced for each station, a factor that adds to production-print costs on :10 ID spots. Some stations will project separately their own call letters while the spots are being run, but this dual projection may detract from the commercial message.

The :20 spot uses :18 of sound, no station identification.

CONSTRUCTING THE :10 ID

Cartoons are particularly effective for the station-break commercial, because they "read" quickly and they can better compete for attention against the surrounding commercials.

The layout of the :10 ID is not simple, since it must work in only 75% of the total area, the left half of the screen and the bottom right quarter, while the upper right 25% is given over to the station call letters. Cartoon simplifies this layout problem.

Dolly shots should be avoided, since camera movement calls unnecessary attention to the station call letters which remain stationary.

Remember, this is "reminder" advertising. The sponsor's name must be firmly identified, along with a slogan or one simple copy point.

Action on the screen is essential, but it is wise to restrict the

140

:10 ID to two scenes and it is sometimes better to stay within a single setting, moving and replacing the component parts. This gives the fluidity needed for this short spot, while direct cuts or dissolves between separate scenes may fracture the impact.

Rule of thumb: Be certain the sponsor's logo is on-screen at least half of the :10 time. Longer, if possible.

SHORT AND SWEET

The :10 ID can be a single spot, repeated ad infinitum, or it can be a "family" series, each bearing a very close resemblance to the other.

Carnation Milk has utilized the ID successfully with a central cartoon character, an animated "Magic Milk Drop", opening each commercial with the wave of a magic wand (a carnation plucked from label) and then demonstrating one usage of the product.

Copy always followed the same format, each opening with a "magic" sound effect:

"Cream your coffee with the milk that whips—
Carnation Evaporated Milk"

"From Contented Cows—for Contented Babies—
Carnation Evaporated Milk"

"Cook with Carnation for appetizing dishes—
Carnation Evaporated Milk"

Animation was simple, effective, as the carnation wand conjured up the graphic coffee cup, baby's bottle or baked casserole. Much of the same animation was later incorporated in :20 and 1:00 spots for Carnation and also used on the Burns & Allen show. This made the IDs doubly effective as "reminder" copy.

Another formula used effectively in a "family" series of IDs was developed by Edelweiss Beer. One copy line served four spots, each of which had different opening animation. The audio:

141

> WOMAN: "What a man won't do for Edelweiss brew!"
>
> ANNOUNCER: "Finest Edelweiss in its 100-year history!"

Such similarity in ID series is a distinct advantage for repetitive impact.

CONSTRUCTION OF THE :20

All the rules that apply for the construction of the 1:00 spot apply for the :20. Just select the dominant sales point and polish that point to its sharpest.

In writing, it is better to write the :20 version first. Then you can later make this a part of the 1:00. If you have done your job right in the shorter version, the minute then will readily permit elaboration and repetition, or the possible addition of secondary sales points. Often it takes two or even three separate :20s to cover the same material that goes into a single 1:00 spot.

In reviewing scripts or completed spots, it is best to study the :20s before the 1:00s to see if construction is sound and if the story has been completely told in the shorter version. If the 1:00 is studied first, the mind may automatically carry over and attribute unincluded material to the :20.

The :20 is an ideal length for the cartoon singing jingle and, as such, it makes a good opening or closing for the 1:00 film.

One of the long-run spots of television was developed by 7-Eleven Stores in Dallas. Their :20 cartoon jingle ran over 4,800 times in a single market area—and the public asked for it back on TV when it was temporarily taken off!

This :20 not only ran as a separate spot, but served as the closing segment of a series of ten 1:00 spots. Each of these ten spots featured individual products or services of the stores, with the cartoon jingle itself being institutional in nature. The popularity of the jingle served to hold the audience through the first :40 of the minute spots so that they could again see the favored :20 closing.

SUCCESS STORIES

The station-break spots have many success stories to their credit. They do pack power.

The Tea Council, using primarily :20 spots and a few 1:00s —*with no other form of advertising*—jumped national sales 11% the first year.

Viceroy Cigarettes upped sales 500% in spot markets with the :20.

Benrus Watch and National Biscuit are two of many other advertisers who have done strong selling jobs with the :20.

Benrus reported in *Television* magazine this formula for buying:

1. Buy 5 or 6 spots per week on a station and hold for year 'round use.
2. Seek 8-10:30 p.m. time to reach the entire family. Adjacencies to better shows preferred.
3. Considering the station's market and Benrus sales in that market, buy up to the amount necessary to get the job done.

Budget: Over $1,000,000 for 63 markets.

Nabisco used a similar budget and a similar number of stations, switching to this spot campaign after previous use of TV programming. The reason, according to George Oliva, advertising director:

"We feel we get more coverage in spot. Spot's flexibility will let us handle different sales problems in each local area. Thus we know that we can adjust our commercials for the South, which favors vanilla wafers, and the West, which favors graham crackers."

So . . . you *can* do the job with the :20 and the :10 ID. Minutes are fine and the prestige of a program is wonderful. But don't think the longer TV time is necessary. Remember a lot of print advertisers have succeeded without using full-page ads. And in television, the screen size is identical, whether your spot is 1:00 or :20 or :10!

DO plan your staging of the ID so as to fully use the left
half and bottom half (that adds up to only 75%) of the
screen. Station call letters must be printed in upper right.
Try to stage the ID in only one or two scenes.

144

DON'T use center staging for the :10 ID — such as you would for the :20. This was permissible when this "Reddy Kilowatt" series was made, but TV stations now require the upper right quarter of the screen for their call letters, visually.

145

DO stage the :20 so that the product is on the screen early and often. Cartoon is ideal for these short spots, but it is wise to use live action or photo animation intercuts to complete your sales story. Here the product is in photo.

146

DON'T waste time with a "story". If you close your eyes and let the bull run away, you'll never get your :20 selling job done. Cartoon is fine to win interest—but be certain you also get your product on the screen within five seconds.

CHAPTER 15

The Writer:

Man With Four Heads

THE WRITER is the one man who can prevent most failures in the development of a television commercial.

He cannot guarantee success, but he can cut down the hazards of the two prime problems of the business: budget and interpretation. He can control costs within his typewriter and he can avoid faulty interpretation through the clarity of his script.

Actually, the TV commercial writer needs to be a "man with four heads." Specifically, he should understand:

1. *Creative Writing,* and the translation of ideas in terms of audience viewpoint.
2. *Advertising,* and the selling needs of this particular advertiser.
3. *Film Production Techniques,* and their physical application to the TV commercial.
4. *Budget Control,* and the pre-set limitations for this script, allowing for film costs, union craftsmanship and the 1953 SAG talent code.

The writer *must* know the first two items and his value will increase in proportion to his knowledge of the next two items. The agency TV director generally stands by with the essential knowledge of items #3 and #4 and he can double-check the writer, but this means *re*-writing the script if the writer has misused his production technique or squandered his budget.

THE WRITER

The writer, as pointed out in Chapter 2, should be the quarterback of the team. He must know the needs and functions of every man on the team and have enough related experience to best conceive the work that will achieve the greatest potential for each—within the budget!

CREATIVE WRITING

Creative writing is the communication of ideas with imagination. To communicate any idea you must know your audience and you must use words and pictures they will readily understand.

This is true in any of the many forms of creative writing. In television, where the potential for imagery is greater, and the audience is broader, this communication of ideas requires explicit knowledge of the people to be reached. This may be partly intuitive, partly schooled.

The writer must understand the viewer or the viewer will not understand the message. The writer's own taste is no criterion. He must know how his viewer lives, what his viewer experiences, to bridge the gap of communication.

This knowledge must then be schooled in the needs of advertising, and the limitations and potentials of film production. Then it becomes *trained* creative writing.

ADVERTISING'S NEEDS

Good advertising copy is the same in all media: it should be simple, human and persuasive.

Simple, easy-to-understand words make it easy to believe, hard to forget. The human factor depends upon the writer's understanding of his audience. The persuasive power is the selling job itself.

These are fundamentals of all good advertising copy.

Good television writing adds another point: it should be graphic. Remember that any scene can be portrayed in at least half-a-dozen ways. It is up to the writer to select the most graphic manner for each scene.

His advertising writing is dependent upon his knowledge of the product, market and consumer research. He must be thoroughly grounded in the sponsor's copy platform and know the sponsor's policies and phobias. He must study competing products. Generally, he must coordinate television with the printed media campaign.

He must realize that the fine phrases of magazine advertising are often ridiculous on TV. Literary style can be a distinct disadvantage. Never can he be "as clever as he can." And he must never get so wrapped up in writing he forgets what he is selling.

In other words, the writer must begin with facts and, using his trained creative ability, end with graphic sales ideas.

THE ART DIRECTOR AND TV DIRECTOR

Good writing in a television commercial is as much on the video side as the audio. Each scene must visualize as the idea is developed step-by-step. Sight and sound must be interlocked and it is vital to remember that the sight is sight-in-motion.

The art director, in many agencies, has become the writer's audio-visual teammate. This can be an ideal arrangement if the art director has a sound working knowledge of item #3: Film Production Techniques.

In such cases, the art director needs to participate in the planning stages, before the script and story-board stages, and his ability to visualize may extend to the selection of settings, props and costuming for the actual production.

General production responsibility centers on the agency TV director, in most operations, and close collaboration with the writer often is indicated. Success generally demands that one or the other have complete understanding of the four items in question, as far as creation of the script is concerned. When the film goes into production, the agency TV director then must successfully interpret the writer's ideas, if he has full responsibility.

It is the faulty interpretation of the writer's conception that causes most production miscarriages in this business. Competent art directors and TV directors collaborating in the creative stages can do much to increase the chances of success.

151

THE WRITER

THE "THIRD" COLUMN

Where the writer does not have the immediate collaboration of the art director or TV director in scripting, it is doubly important that he describe each scene so clearly that no one can misinterpret.

Here is where the writer must have knowledge of item #3: Film Production Techniques, so that he can write out detailed instructions on camera and action. Casting and setting might also be given elaboration so that all who read the script have identical conceptions. This is especially important when someone other than the art director is to draw the story-board.

It is often good to write a script in 3 columns, the "third column" to analyze and explain objectives and to elaborate on the handling desired in the video and audio columns.

When the script comes out of his typewriter, the writer should know the cost of producing the commercial, within 10%. He should be able to clearly explain what his objectives were—in overall and in each scene—and the reasons he has selected the techniques to be employed. And he must know he is getting a worthwhile return for every production dollar to be expended.

It is well to add a "third column" to TV commercial scripts. Also, as shown at the left, a "third panel" to story-boards.

This extra column and panel give the writer of the commercial a full opportunity to explain and analyze his objectives in each scene.

Such "Explanation and Analysis" helps to clarify the writer's basic concept so that all who read—and particularly the other creative craftsmen who interpret the script — will have the identical interpretation.

The parade is now under way. We
cut to this closeup of the Pack
marching at the head of the
Coupons. The Pack and Coupons
are photographic reproductions,
the arms and legs and the rest
of the scene cartoon animation.
The scene is bright and gay and
moves with zip and pep.

VIDEO: Technique: Fotan Animation   Panel # 2

AUDIO: Scene # 1

SINGERS & BAND (con't):

   "King-size Raleighs give you 3

PACK STETCHES OUT 3 FINGERS.

   "King-size extras...Yessiree!

    --Flavor! --Coupons! --Value!

   Golly!..."

THE WRITER

BUDGET CONTROL

It is always best for the writer to work to a given budget.

Many writers can turn out brilliant "ideas"—but with no predetermined knowledge of cost. The television commercial writer who just has "ideas", without planned cost control, is an expensive luxury to any sponsor.

The experienced writer learns to avoid costly scenes in his overall planning because he knows subsequent price-cutting surgery on that scene might emasculate the whole script.

It is not simple for the creative writer to clutter his brains with an adding machine, but the good ones have, the others must.

Further, the writer now must have a complete knowledge of the workings of the 1953 SAG talent code. He must know how much and how often the talent payments and repayments run. Careless attention to this detail can cost the sponsor many times his actual production investment.

FOUR HEADS WITH THEIR NECKS STUCK OUT

So the writer has to be a creative craftsman—actually a psychologist, salesman, film craftsman and accountant.

Not enough credit is given to most agency writers—and certainly not enough authority. The writer should be in all planning sessions. When the script is ready for production, he should also be in all briefing sessions with the producer's staff, for these are the men who will interpret his ideas. Whenever possible, the writer should be on the set and in all the phases of the production operation.

It is through such practical experience that he prepares himself to do his next job better. If he has been working with the art director or the agency TV director, he will gain a better conception of their jobs and so improve in collaboration.

Faulty communication remains the persistent hazard of the business. The writer can save his salary times over by preventing this confusion.

Good writing is the surest insurance against extravagance and waste in television commercials.

154

A DOZEN DO'S AND DONT'S OF
GOOD TV COMMERCIAL WRITING:

The most common mistakes in writing for television commercials would be found somewhere in these twelve Dont's. As antidotes, a dozen Do's follow:

1. Don't start without complete preparation.
    Do learn your product, your market, your viewer, your budget.

2. Don't jump right into a sales pitch.
    Do win viewer interest in the first few seconds. Get his eyes and ears—and *mind*—on your message.

3. Don't confuse with too many sales points.
    Do stay with one central idea, build it up logically —that's television's advantage of control in step-by-step salesmanship.

4. Don't write too much audio.
    Do keep within the speed of viewer understanding. For most purposes: 130-155 words per minute.

5. Don't write too little audio.
    Do keep interest sustained, once you have won it. Work for combined sight-sound impact.

6. Don't cut scenes too short.
    Do set a minimum of 3 seconds for the viewer to fully orient himself to any new scene.

7. Don't run scenes too long.
    Do use the rule-of-thumb, that, after 6 seconds, "something better move—or the viewer will."

8. Don't write exclusively for the eye; the viewer can't come back and look at it, as in a magazine.
    Do write for complete understanding; the audio should make clear what the video does not quickly explain.

155

9. Don't play tricks on your audience.

> Do be honest in winning interest—keep it relevant—and be honest in demonstration and use of so-called "camera tricks."

10. Don't confuse with too many scenes, or "too busy" scenes.

> Do keep all settings simple, without distractions from your sales story.

11. Don't use too many actors.

> Do keep basic casts small. One or two persons can ingratiate themselves to the audience faster, more personally, than a group. Also, remember the SAG talent re-payments.

12. Don't skimp on video instructions.

> Do describe each scene fully and completely. If necessary, write a third column to explain your objectives and how you believe each scene should be handled.

THE WRITER'S SIX I-CHECKS OF A COMMERCIAL:

There are six needs of a television commercial which "I" must check. The first two factors have to do with planning; the second two are the factors that gain an audience; the last two are factors that sell the audience. Remember it this way:

IN PLANNING:
I need first the sales *idea*—
Then I need to develop this *idea* with *imagination*.

IN GAINING VIEWERS:
I need first to win the viewer's *interest*—
Then I need to answer that *interest* with *information*.

IN SELLING VIEWERS:
I need first to interlock the *idea* with the product for *identification*—
Then I need this *identification* interlocked with both sight and sound for *impact!*

Check and re-check! Yes, the most successful commercials are able to pass these six I-checks before they reach the screen:

IDEA AND IMAGINATION
INTEREST AND INFORMATION
IDENTIFICATION AND IMPACT

DO switch to cartoon for that comic situation if it must be used in your commercial. The exaggerated pose, action and sound effects of cartoon tell the story faster and funnier. Animation directors are well schooled in the comic situation.

DON'T break your neck trying to stage live actors in comic situations. Comedy is a tough, hard business and rarely "comes off" in live action commercials, certainly not without actors and directors long experienced in the art. Do you *have* to be funny?

DO rely on props and situation rather than people if you must have humor in live action. And be certain to distinguish between the humor of a situation and an outright attempt at comedy. You laugh *with* humor; you laugh *at* comedy. It is a risky field in live action commercials, at best!

160

DON'T try to extract comedy from established traditional concepts. It is true that April Fool's cards have encroached on Valentine's Day and more recently the Christmas season, but don't make the mistake of trying to do this with TV commercials. Never risk offending traditional concepts "sacred" to viewers.

161

1 — ANNCR: (OFF SCREEN) "We take you now to Hollywood for a word from a famous screen star . . .

2 — " . . . 's garbage can". DOWAGER TYPE CARTOON CAN: "I just want to say a word to garbage cans everywhere:

3 — "Do you offend socially? Are you troubled with pesky flies?

4 — "You needn't be! Use 20 Mule Team Borax . . . and you'll never risk offending!"

5 — ROSEMARY: (LAUGHS) "The little cartoon is right! You women who already know how effective Borax is for sweetening laundry will welcome this new use. Directions are right on the box.

6 — (CLOSEUP BOX) "See what its says?" DOWAGER CAN: "Yes, why don't you get an *extra* package of 20 Mule Team Borax . . . and keep it handy!"

CHAPTER 16

About BELIEVABILITY: Psychologically, we know it is necessary to establish one believable scene before the viewer is ready to believe subsequent claims. Perhaps Alka-Seltzer has done this job better than anyone else. They say: "Drop a tablet in the water— listen to it FIZZ! Drink it—you'll feel better."

When a customer drops an Alka-Seltzer in the water, it *does* FIZZ. He believes it. Then he drinks it—and feels better! Psychology at work, both in advertising and in actual practice.

* * *

About CASTING: TV commercials should receive casting that is different from motion pictures or even TV entertainment films. There is greater need for not-too-handsome faces with "character" that quickly win viewers. There is less need for the too-pretty girl. In a magazine ad, the reader can casually change his interest from the pretty girl to the copy—but in television he simply doesn't have time to shift gears.

* * *

About CLOSEUPS: Use generously: Closeups are more personal, more vivid, more effective . . . and cheaper!

* * *

About COLOR: With the advent of color, there arises a vast number of pseudo experts, even as in the swaddling days of black-and-white TV. In the end, to avoid the same bumbling, it seems the industry must turn to the color film production men who have a quarter of a century of related experience. Nothing, however, will avoid the increased problems that color introduces to nearly every phase of television.

Make no mistake, color is something that shouldn't have happened to the still-growing industry for another five years.

* * *

About EDUCATIONAL FILMS: We believe that educational films soon will borrow new-found knowledge from the television commercial field. Good advertising educates. And educational and propaganda films already can take notes on advertising's first half-dozen years in TV.

* * *

About EXAGGERATING THE EXAGGERATED CLAIM: A copy man at BBDO says: "You can't say anything about a 25¢ cigar that someone hasn't already said about a 5¢ cigar".

* * *

About "FATIGUED RESPONSE": A fortune awaits the man who can accurately compute the point at which the audience will cease to respond favorably to a hit tune or a singing jingle or a previously successful TV spot. This is the point when a thing has been seen or heard too often—it no longer happily jars the mind. This is the "yawn point" at which you need to have a switcheroo ready. Researchers Gallup & Robinson take the view that a commercial does not necessarily lose its effectiveness through constant repetition, but Social Research differs: "The fifth time that a pretty girl drools identically over the same pretty man with the same tender sensuous endorsement of his shaving cream, the whole thing takes on a mechanical quality and the warm emotional impact is not only gone, but is replaced by a negative response."

166

DO get expert help in attempting live color commercials. Settings, costuming, art direction, makeup, camera work, processing all require greater skills—and more time! Color live action should cost only about 20-30% more than similar material in black-and-white, but there will be many costly exceptions.

RANDOM OBSERVATIONS

About FILM BIDS: We are inclined to predict that film bids in the future will be required only on a minority of commercials. Instead, the agency will set the budget and then select the producer. There is every reason for such a plan, once agency TV directors master their business and win the confidence of their suppliers for fair dealing. Sales costs for some commercial producers now run as high as 35%—which means *every third dollar* never reaches the screen. Such an agency-producer plan would eliminate this waste.

* * *

About LIVE COMMERCIALS: As the Introduction warned, this book has been primarily concerned with *film*, since 4 out of 5 of the TV spots used by major agencies are on film. For those rugged individualists of Madison Avenue who still argue for the "spontaneity" of live television commercials and for those equally hardy souls who must buck the trend because of time, budget or peculiar problems, we recommend you avoid Chapters 7 and 9-through-14. But there is ample fuel for your fire in Chapters 1-through-5 and 8. Especially 8!

* * *

About MEMORY DEVICES: In Chapter 4 of this book, you'll find "S—A—L—E" and "I—D—E—A—$". Another of our favorite memory devices is "the vowels of good advertising":

A — Attain interest
E — Express a promise
I — Identify the promise with the product
O — Organize sales facts
U — Urge to buy

But Chet Glassley puts it more succinctly for television advertising. He calls his formula the "4-L evaluation": The viewer must "Look at it, Listen to it, Like it—and then get the L out and latch on to it!"

* * *

About MOVIE STAR TESTIMONIALS: A research report on public acceptance of testimonials concludes: "The impression appears to be widely held that movie stars will give a testimonial for almost any product, provided they are paid enough to do so. When the movie star's testimonial is disbelieved rather than accepted, this is a liability."

* * *

About MOVIE THEATER ADVERTISING: This subject is worthy of an extra chapter, but space does not permit. Movie advertising ties in perfectly with the television commercial, and is especially good for manufacturer-dealer campaigns or any localized selling.

Color originals can be made for theater use, with black-and-white prints for TV. Ford, Bendix, Tappan Range and dozens of other sponsors now employ Theater-TV dual-usage with success. Some 15,000 theaters now run color commercials. About 3500 of these are drive-ins. According to recent figures, 120 national accounts and 50,000 local accounts now advertise in theaters.

It is an ideal medium to intensify or supplement TV.

* * *

About the NEED FOR KNOWLEDGE: Advertising has not trained enough competent people for television commercial work. Special schools and seminars are needed. Stan Lomas of Esty agency reports: "We have interviewed over 450 hopefuls in 3 years and found 1% qualified by experience or aptitude. Genuine TV commercial experience is scarce."

* * *

About OPTICALS: Trick opticals are still overdone in TV commercials and viewers are still saying "How'd they do that?" when they might better be absorbing the message. Keep it simple. Particularly avoid "split-screens" and montages which confuse the viewer. Show one thing at a time in normal, natural closeup.

* * *

About POPULARITY: It is interesting to note why the viewers like or dislike a commercial, as reported in a survey by Advertest:

Like, because: "music", "central character", "cartoon", "easy to understand", "informative", "story line".

Carnation Milk hits Negro and Mexican markets with special theater color ad films. In Negro films, Freda de-Knight, foods editor of EBONY Magazine, is featured. More than 500 theaters have dominantly Negro audiences.

170

Coca-Cola has used theater advertising for more than 20 years. Good public relations is done by such series as *Let's Visit America* with cartoon tours of the states, ending on a "Coca-Cola is everywhere . . ." theme. Here was South Carolina.

RANDOM OBSERVATIONS

Dislike, because: "repetition", "too much talk", "extravagant claims", "untruthfulness", "artificial sounding".

There is some meat in this, but remember that like or dislike is not your primary objective. It's a case of sell or not sell! You're not running a popularity contest.

* * *

About RESEARCH "AUTHORITIES": It seems necessary to challenge some of the statements given out by advertising research groups that now turn their talents to the TV commercial. For instance:

"Turn off the sound—if it's still good, it's good TV." Such a test for a commercial is intriguing, but too many jingles, effect tracks and other successful commercials seem to disprove it. You wouldn't test a car by driving it on only two wheels, would you?

"Opening interest is not needed." This conclusion apparently was reached in closed theater tests before captive audiences. Can it be true in actual television broacasting? If so, why do advertising men rack their brains for the "opening interest" illustration or headline in a print ad?

* * *

About SCREENING FINAL PRINTS: When the film commercial is completed and screened for the agency and advertiser, it is well to restrict the audience only to those persons who have had an active part in the planning and production of the script—those who are completely conversant with the advertising objectives in mind. If too many "appointed critics" are asked their opinions, controversies will arise and second-guessing suggestions will thwart the original aims.

* * *

About SETTINGS: Bea Adams of Gardner, recent "Advertising Woman of the Year," has sound advice for the handling of mass market products (like her own Pet Milk and Ralston): "When it comes to setting and props . . . use a Sears catalogue." Look at a modern Sears store or catalog and you'll see what she means.

* * *

About SIMILARITY: It would seem that viewers might

172

be confused with the similarity of competing commercials in the watch, cosmetic, beer and automotive fields. Rival spots use the same optical tricks, the same camera angles, the same type jingles and similar testimonials. Is it possible that such similarity indicates to the viewer that the products themselves are also so similar there is no difference between them?

Bill Millard of McCann-Erickson phrases this with a warning: "Where many brands of the same product make the claim of superiority, there is some reason for scepticism as to the truth of such claims. Since the poor viewer does not know which *one* advertiser to believe, he ends by being suspicious of *all*."

* * *

About SMOKING AND EATING: It is interesting to compare a typical month's network revenue from television advertising. All food products combined accounted for $5,103,578, as against $3,556,263 for smoking materials and $3,520,959 for cosmetics.

* * *

About "TEST" FILMS: There have been various attempts to produce mock-up commercials, simulating the finished product in advance. Then these are run before private audiences and tested for recall of copy points and memory factors.

The value of such "testing" should be challenged where talent and production values are necessary to get basic sales ideas across, such as in the case of cosmetics. These psychological factors are bound to be lacking in the cheap test film.

However, testing of commercials, especially finished film commercials, can be useful in the hands of competent research analysts. Coupled with skilled deep-probing interviews, such tests can indicate comparative attention value, believability, recall and probable sales effectiveness.

The trick is to *interpret* the data, and here the agency perspective is essential.

173

RANDOM OBSERVATIONS

About THE VIEWER: NBC came up with some interesting conclusions in *TV Today* (1952). Here is their story on TV set owners:

1. The longer they own TV, the more TV advertising they recall.
2. The more they watch TV, the more TV advertising they recall.
3. The more they watch TV, the more they buy TV brands.
4. The better they like the program, the better the advertising is received.
5. TV owners vote 2-1 TV is the most convincing ad medium.
6. Non-owners also consider TV the most convincing.
7. The more they watch the more they consider TV convincing.

* * *

About THE SAME: NBC came up with more interesting conclusions in *Why Sales Come in Curves* (1953):

1. If they begin viewing, they begin buying.
2. If they stop viewing, they stop buying.
3. If they continue viewing, they continue buying.
4. If they continue not viewing, they continue not buying.

It's as simple as that . . . to hear NBC tell it!

* * *

About Four FINAL QUESTIONS: A good check-list on a script after it is written:

1. Did you supply *useful* information—for the viewer?
2. Did you *demonstrate* reason why—for the product?
3. Did you insure *identification*—for the sponsor?
4. Did you create an *urge to buy*—for the dealer?

174

About YARDSTICKS: There probably isn't a single yardstick or opinionated observation in this book that some good commercial cannot violate and prove exception. No one can fetter creative talent, in art or drama or even in a TV commercial, with rules that cannot be broken successfully. Are you challenged?

* * *

About the FUTURE: Television will still be "growing" ten years from now, and the commercial must lead this change because only by increasing effectiveness can the commercial pay the ever-increasing bill. One agency head predicts that, within five years, 90% of their billing will be in TV. Color and 3-Dimension are coming. Psychological and sociological research will open new doors. Selling power, now barely dreamed of, will develop.

The Future: *unlimited* . . .

PHOTO CREDITS:

Advertisers:

Alka-Seltzer
Armour's Cheese
Borax
Bull Dog Beer
Carnation Milk
Celotex
Chevrolet
Cinch Cake Mix
Coca-Cola
Cory
Delaware Punch
Dickie's Work Clothes
Dodge
Durkee's Margarine
Edelweiss Beer
Elmer's Chee-Wees
Ford
Folger's Coffee
Fuller Paints
Globe A1 Flour
Goebel's Beer
Heinz Soups
Helene Curtis
Hotpoint
Interstate Bakeries
Jergen's Facial
Kellogg's Cereals
Knapp-Monarch
  Appliances
Log Cabin Bread
Lucerne Milk
Lucky Tiger Hair Tonic
Manor House Coffee
Mayrose Meats
Maytag Washers

Muratti Cigarettes
Old Judge Coffee
Pabst Blue Ribbon Beer
Pet Milk
Peter Pan Peanut Butter
Pfeiffer's Beer
Rain Drops Water
  Softener
Raleigh Cigarettes
Ralston
Reed's Candy
7-Eleven Stores
Sheaffer Pens
S.O.S. Scouring Pads
Soil-Off
Standard Oil
Stokeley's Honor Brand
Swift Eggs
Suave
Tappan Ranges
Tea Council
Union Electric
Wembley Ties
Whitman's Sampler
Wilshire Club Beverages
Zenith Hearing Aids

Agencies:

Batten, Barton, Durstine
  & Osborn, Inc.
Brooke, Smith, French &
  Dorrance, Inc.
Gordon Best Company,
  Inc.
Brisacher, Wheeler &
  Staff, Inc.
Leo Burnett, Inc.
Campbell-Ewald Co.

Stanley Campbell, Adver-
  tising
D'Arcy Advertising Co.
Dancer-Fitzgerald-
  Sample, Inc.
Erwin-Wasey & Co., Ltd.
Evans & Associates
Foote, Cone & Belding
Gardner Advertising
  Company
Grant Advertising
  Agency
Kelso Norman Advertis-
  ing
Earle Ludgin & Co.
MacFarland, Aveyard &
  Co.
Maxon, Inc.
McCann-Erickson, Inc.
Dan B. Miner Company
Needham, Louis &
  Brorby, Inc.
Olian & Bronner Adver-
  tising
Potts-Turnbull Co.
Elwood J. Robinson
Ruthrauff & Ryan, Inc.
Russel M. Seeds Co., Inc.
Stockton, West, Burkhart,
  Inc.
J. Walter Thompson
  Company
Tracy-Locke Company
Geoffrey Wade Adv.
  Agency
Walker-Saussy, Advertis-
  ing
Ward-Wheelock Co.
Warwick & Legler, Inc.